HOW GREEN IS GREEN?

HOW GREEN IS GREEN?

38 EUCHARISTIC CELEBRATIONS FOR TODAY'S YOUTH

Rev. Etienne LeBlanc
and
Sister Mary Rose Talbot, C.I.C.

Ave Maria Press / Notre Dame / Indiana 46556

Acknowledgments

We wish to express our deepest gratitude to Ann Barry for her insights into the musical selections for the liturgies.

We wish also to thank our typists, Mrs. Betty Dugas, Mrs. Jenny Hymel and Miss Carol Rivere; and Father Sidney Becnel and Mrs. Thelma Landry for their insights and encouragement.

Nihil Obstat: John L. Reedy, C.S.C.
Censor Deputatus

Imprimatur: Most Rev. Leo A. Pursley, D.D.
Bishop of Fort Wayne/South Bend

Library of Congress Catalog Card Number: 73-83350
International Standard Book Number: 0-87793-061-9
© Ave Maria Press, Notre Dame, Indiana. All rights reserved
Printed in the United States of America
Art: Cathy Chenez

"God purposely chose what the world considers nonsense in order to put wise men to shame."
                                    1 Corinthians 1:27

To the children of St. Peter's and
Our Lady of Prompt Succor Schools.

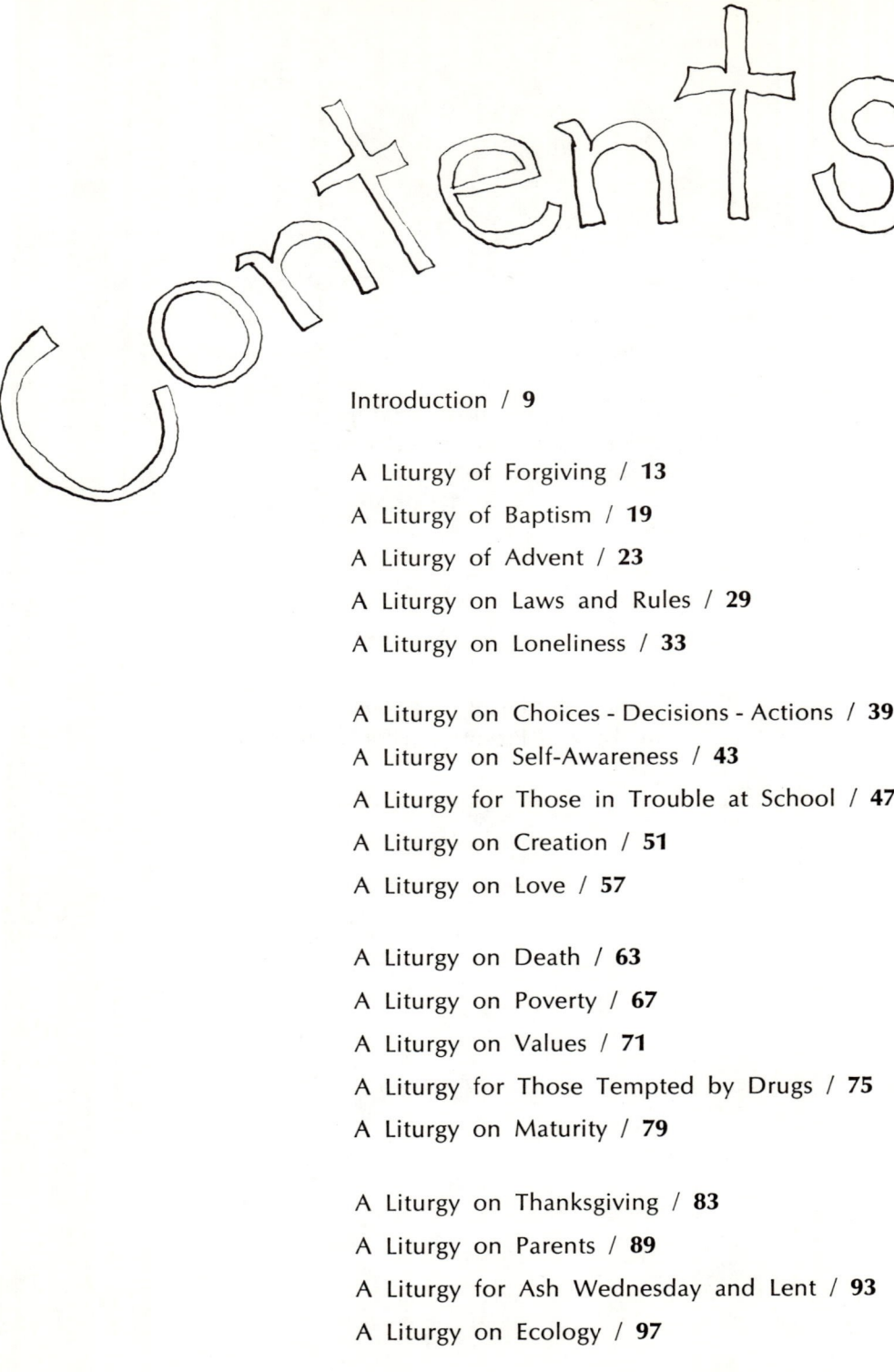

Contents

Introduction / **9**

A Liturgy of Forgiving / **13**
A Liturgy of Baptism / **19**
A Liturgy of Advent / **23**
A Liturgy on Laws and Rules / **29**
A Liturgy on Loneliness / **33**

A Liturgy on Choices - Decisions - Actions / **39**
A Liturgy on Self-Awareness / **43**
A Liturgy for Those in Trouble at School / **47**
A Liturgy on Creation / **51**
A Liturgy on Love / **57**

A Liturgy on Death / **63**
A Liturgy on Poverty / **67**
A Liturgy on Values / **71**
A Liturgy for Those Tempted by Drugs / **75**
A Liturgy on Maturity / **79**

A Liturgy on Thanksgiving / **83**
A Liturgy on Parents / **89**
A Liturgy for Ash Wednesday and Lent / **93**
A Liturgy on Ecology / **97**

A Liturgy on Celebrating / **103**
A Liturgy on Hope / **107**
A Liturgy on Sharing / **111**
A Liturgy on Speaking / **115**
A Liturgy on the Ascension / **119**

A Liturgy on Freedom / **123**
A Liturgy on Listening / **127**
A Liturgy on Time / **131**
A Liturgy on Epiphany / **135**
A Liturgy for Halloween and Saints' Days / **139**

A Liturgy for Pentecost / **145**
A Liturgy on Witness / **149**
A Liturgy on Prejudice / **153**
A Liturgy on Peace / **157**
A Liturgy for Beginning School / **161**

A Liturgy for Teachers / **165**
A Liturgy for Discovery / **169**
A Liturgy on Receiving-Accepting / **173**
A Liturgy for the Closing of School / **177**

Ideas, Anyone? / **181**

PUBLISHER'S NOTE

Customs and regulations regarding liturgical practice vary widely in different localities. Yet there is a very real need for creative source material from which selections can be made in fashioning liturgies for special groups and special occasions. The suggestions in this book are offered to serve that need in the area of youth liturgies. The particular selections and different approaches suggested may be made use of according to what best fills the need in a particular local situation. Thus, this is a source book which must be adapted to local norms, customs and regulations.

Introduction

WHAT'S IT ALL ABOUT?

For everything there is a season: a time for giving birth, a time for growing. Youth—caught up in an adult world—often asks: "What's it all about?" Adults often answer: "It's about life."

Worship is an "encounter with a mystery that gives meaning to life." But one has to experience liturgy for it to be meaningful. For liturgy to be real, it must "change my life" . . . and that includes my life from 7 to 17.

Liturgies should make children more conscious of themselves as persons and more convinced that true Christianity involves concern for neighbor. Children are active; they love to do things, to be where the action is, to become involved. This "becoming involved" should be part of the child's world of liturgy as well as part of the world of school, teachers, parents, and peers. By seeing himself involved with neighbor and with liturgy, we hope he will see God.

Meaningful worship should give us all an experience of belonging, a sense of "togetherness." There has to be a link between worship and the world around us.

A liturgy on "forgiving." for example, enables a child to realize that he himself as a person and his neighbor are vital factors in his love of God. We should strive always to help young people tolerate, forgive, and love one another. Sin has been defined as "a turning away from God," and it begins when we turn away from our neighbor. Hence the need for experiencing forgiveness in a liturgy. If worship is meaningful, then a young person's life will become meaningful.

What's a good liturgy for youth all about? A good liturgy for youth has a simplified theme, language that carries meaning for that age, and involvement in the liturgy, e.g., by announcing the theme, or taking part in a dialogue homily. A good liturgy employs symbols, for symbols have proved to be a very direct way to the subconscious. Youths' own world is filled with symbols. A good liturgy makes application to the lives of young people and "continues" during the week in the youths' world beyond the place of worship and celebration. It also has a high esteem for scripture both in the liturgy itself and in daily lives.

Finally, good liturgy demands creative effort on the part of planners. It would be a mistake of the highest order to think that meaningful worship is a simple thing to enact, something which just happens. If worship is to be dynamic and revolutionizing in the life of a Christian, then it must be well planned.

A WAY

How green is green? How interested are you in life and liturgy and love? How interested are you in contributing to meaningful worship? Do you really want to help young people experience a depth to reality?

PRACTICAL APPLICATION

Time is a very important element in all our lives—even the apparently timeless wonderworld of children. No one can experience a depth of reality in 40 minutes. The classroom, the home and the community are good places to carry out activities related to the theme of a liturgy. Liturgy should involve as much of the total person as possible; it should correlate itself with the natural interest of the young. There should be related activities during the week that carry out the theme of the liturgy—some type of daily application. Then, perhaps, a youth will begin to realize the place of God in life—in his life, in relation to himself and his peers.

MUSIC

Proper music enhances a liturgy and makes it more meaningful. To choose good, popular music for liturgy you have only to listen to the words and ask: "What is the song saying?" "Does it have a message?" "Does it have any bearing on the liturgy?" "Can everyone sing it?" If the answer is yes, then chances are the songs are good ones.

Instruments help greatly with singing. Guitars, organs, trumpets, tambourines, drums, you-name-it. One word of caution, however: No instrument should be employed in liturgical worship without proper preparation and practice of the music. Where youth are involved, practice should be scheduled; if it isn't, there may be no practice at all.

Since music is a "disposable art," there is a great need to continue to learn new songs as they are being written, and to keep up with a study of music that makes it possible to have good liturgies. So often we hear "Where can I get the record?" or "Where can I buy the music?" Popular recordings from music stores lend themselves to meaningful worship. Having a "music-share-in" with other people in the community or neighboring community is an excellent opportunity for the young to share their music technique and learn new things from others. Music is a medium that has universal appeal. But it is a mistake to think it must be played all the time, or always sung. Some music may be listened to, or played as accompaniment while showing slides or films. The key to good music for liturgy is the courage and conviction that good liturgy is worth your effort and your time.

SCRIPTURE

The most basic book of all spirituality is scripture, but too often it is forgotten. The bible should be the most esteemed and used source of spiritual formation. If the child is to model his life on the life of Jesus . . . if the teachings of Jesus are to be considered a value, then a child must come into personal contact with the person of Jesus in the bible.

To place the bible in its proper perspective, a short reading could be assigned every day of the week. The scripture passages can be read in the classroom by a teacher, at some appropriate time of the day, with some explanation. The students can also give their understanding of the passage. Some time should be allowed for private reflection or meditation. Perhaps it would be possible to choose a particular student or group of students to present the reading to the class and explain what the passage means to them. Another approach would include individual private reading and reflection, followed by group or class discussion. An alternative to this method could involve allowing the students to act out the scripture reading. Any one of these approaches helps the scriptures come alive.

BANNERS

Banners are a visual reminder of a message. If used and displayed properly, banners can be very effective tools in liturgical services. Banner making need not be costly; it can be done with inexpensive material, things like contact paper and burlap. A short message is the best; too many words on a banner make it unreadable. Young people should be encouraged to make their own banners. After the services, the banner should be hung in a conspicuous place —perhaps in the school where all the students can see it.

SHARING

We have attempted briefly to show the need for involving the *total* person in liturgical worship, worship that will give meaning to the person's life as a Christian. The rest of this book contains examples of experimental liturgies that were compiled for use with students. The liturgies were based on themes that, we hope, make worship more meaningful to young people, and add a "depth to their world of reality." It is our sincerest hope that they will be helpful. As in all cases of experimentation, we can only create "an atmosphere and hope that you have an experience."

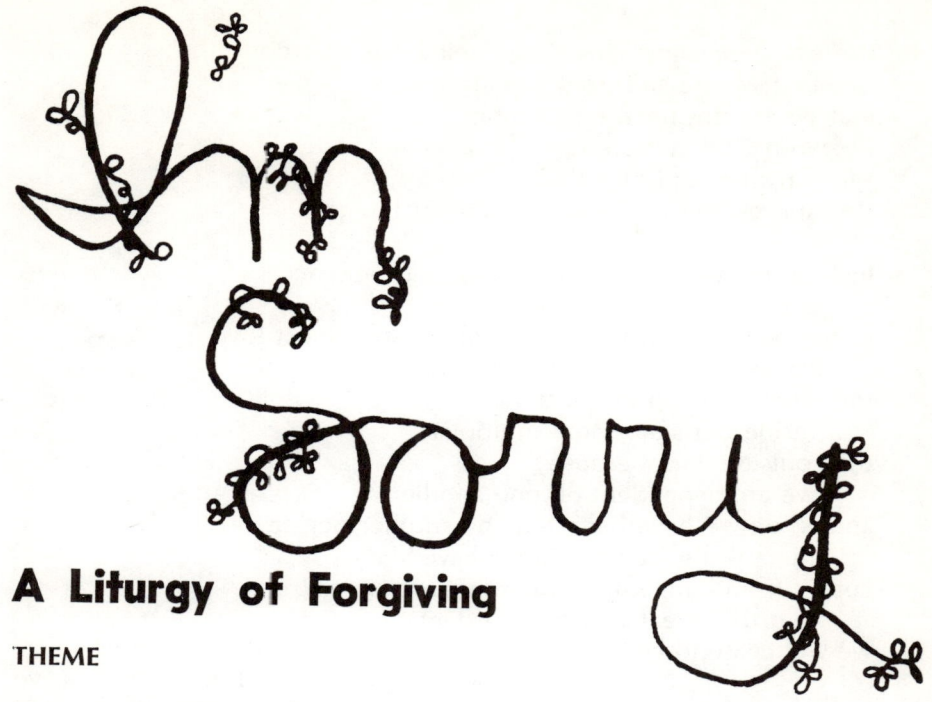

A Liturgy of Forgiving

THEME

(The theme for the day's liturgy may be read by a student or announced by the celebrant.)

We must be friends to each other here as Jesus was our friend; and today we want to forgive each other as Jesus forgives us. We will think about all the things we have done that made us unfriendly to other people.

ORDER OF CELEBRATION

A) The celebrant enters the church in silence.

B) Celebrant reads an appropriate prayer on forgiveness.

> "Father, we come together here to ask you to let us look at ourselves as we are, and we ask your help to be better.
> Through Christ our Lord. Amen."

C) Everyone is seated and there is an appropriate reading on forgiveness.

The Hurt of Sin

> God's gift of relationship with him
>   and with one another,
> With all that it promises of fulfillment,
>   is denied us by our sin.

We can understand this sin as being our assertion
   that we are sufficient of ourselves,
that we do not need relationship
   with God or man.
We fear men and hurt them
   and exploit not only persons but things.

Indeed, the worst hurt any of us can experience
   is the hurt suffered at the hands
of someone we love and from whom we expect love.
   Personal hurts hurt on the inside;
the others hurt on the outside.
   Inside hurts are more injurious
than outside ones because
   we are dependent on one another;
and when we have been hurt by another person,
   there is the feeling that we have been
cut off from him, with the consequent anxiety
   that to a greater or lesser extent
we will cease to be.

          (Reuel L. Howe, quoted in *Listen To Love*
          by Louis M. Savary, S.J., The Regina
          Press, Hicksville, N.Y. 11801, 1970.)

D) The celebrant then asks the students to participate in the penitential rite by naming some things they should like forgiveness for.

(The celebrant should stand near the students for this service, and he should be the first to respond.)

E) After the penitential rite, everyone sings an appropriate hymn.
E.g.—"Yes Lord." (May use forward motion of the hands whenever these words are sung.)

F) **GOSPEL READING:** Luke 17:3,4

G) **HOMILY AND PRACTICAL ASPECTS:**
The purpose of this liturgy is to make children more conscious of taking back into their friendship those whom they have slighted, disobeyed or injured in any way. The need to forgive is mutual. The song "Love One Another" may be used in developing a dialogue homily with children.

    MONDAY — During the morning recess show someone that you are sorry by inviting him to play in your game.

TUESDAY	— Help your mother at home.
WEDNESDAY	— Let someone get in front of you for water at the drinking fountain.
THURSDAY	— Invite someone to play at your home.
FRIDAY	— Do something nice for the teacher.

H) **LITURGY OF THE EUCHARIST NOW TAKES PLACE**

Prayer Over the Gifts

"Father, we place our gifts of bread and wine and ourselves before you, knowing well that we have all done wrong. We pray that you will come among us in the Body and Blood of Christ. We ask this through Christ our Lord. Amen."

Prayer After Communion

"Father, we thank you for our receiving Jesus in Communion and also for your words 'I forgive you and love you.' For this we are filled with thanks and will do our best to make our thanks real in the way we live in the days of this week.
Through Christ our Lord. Amen."

SUGGESTED SONGS FOR LITURGY OF FORGIVING

1. Penitential Rite: "Yes, Lord"
2. Offertory: "Service"
3. Communion hymn: "Love One Another"
4. Recessional: "Peace, My Friends"

AFTER THE LITURGY

Banner — possible quotes — *(Banners, when used, should be brought into the church and hung in a conspicuous place.)*

1. Forgive and try to forget.
2. Some get and forget; others give and forgive.

Application in School

The practical application of this liturgy of forgiving to the lives of the students could be effectively carried out with the help of teachers. Anything that teachers or students wish to do to make this theme meaningful should be highly encouraged. The following are samples:

1. The banner should be hung in a conspicuous place in the school as a reminder of the theme for the week.

2. A child should be appointed to make a copy of the daily application suggestions given by the students during the liturgical celebration; and this should be posted in the room as a reminder to the students of what has been suggested.

3. One student should place a poster with the daily application in the school, perhaps next to the banner. The poster should be changed every day.

Biblical Readings

All children should be highly encouraged to read scripture. This is a source of "God revealing himself to us." Those bible translations which are more suitable for children should be used.

We recommend a short reading every day on the liturgical theme. This reading may be done by the teacher or, preferably, by the students silently. A few minutes should be given for reflection.

Some suggested readings for the week:

MONDAY — Mark 2:2-5
TUESDAY — Matthew 9:8
WEDNESDAY — Matthew 16:19 and 18:18
THURSDAY — Matthew 5:24
FRIDAY — Matthew 18:23-25

VARIATIONS

Penitential Rite:

For failing to remember that we ourselves and all we have are your gifts to us,

LORD HAVE MERCY

For failing to respect our parents and all others whose love makes them care about us,

CHRIST HAVE MERCY

For taking what doesn't belong to us or being selfish with what we have,

LORD HAVE MERCY

Gospel reading: Luke 23:33,34
Epistle reading: 1 Peter 3:8-12

NOTES:
_____
_____
_____
_____
_____
_____
_____
_____
_____
_____

A Liturgy on Baptism

THEME

Baptism is our birth as Christians. Because we are all baptized into the family of Christ, there should be no arguments or fights or anything else that would be uncharitable. God's presence in us should shake us out of our sleepy selves and make us truly alive and free Christians—holy people. Today we will think of our baptisms and try to become alive Christians.

ORDER OF CELEBRATION

A) The celebrant enters the church, accompanied by a server carrying a large candle. This candle is placed on the altar and only this candle is used during the celebration. An appropriate hymn is sung during the procession. The other server carries a glass bowl with holy water and places it on a table in the center aisle.

B) **PENITENTIAL RITE:**

> For not giving to a brother in need,
>> LORD HAVE MERCY

> For not listening to your word in the bible,
>> CHRIST HAVE MERCY

> For not loving others enough,
>> LORD HAVE MERCY

C) **AN APPROPRIATE PRAYER IS READ:**

"Father, we are your children, born again of water and your Spirit in the promise of Jesus rising; help us to grow in your Spirit because there is no standing still—the leaf grows green or falls brown."

D) **FIRST READING:**

"In baptism we use your gift of water, which you have made a rich symbol of the grace you give us in this sacrament.

"At the very dawn of creation your Spirit breathed on the waters, making them the wellspring of all holiness. The waters of the great flood you made a sign of the waters of baptism, that make an end of sin and a new beginning of goodness. Through the waters of the Red Sea you led Israel out of slavery, to be an image of God's holy people, set free from sin by baptism. In the waters of the Jordan your Son was baptized by John and anointed with the Spirit. Your Son willed that water and blood should flow from his side as he hung upon the cross. After his resurrection he told his disciples: 'Go out and teach all nations, baptizing them in the name of the Father, and of the Son, and of the Holy Spirit.'"

(The Rite of Baptism)

E) **GOSPEL READING:** Matthew 28:18-20

F) **HOMILY AND PRACTICAL ASPECTS:**

The homily should take place near the dish of holy water that was placed in the center aisle. It should review in a dialogical manner the sacrament of baptism which the children received when they were infants. At the conclusion of the homily, students should be told they can mark themselves with the sign of the cross using holy water from this dish as a reminder of their baptism and as a pledge of greater commitment to Christianity. Some practical aspects of the homily for the week could be:

MONDAY — When you go home today, ask your parents to tell you everything that happened at your baptism. Bring out your baptismal pictures and take a look at them.

TUESDAY — Write, with the help of your teacher, what it means to be a Christian.

WEDNESDAY — Today say special prayers to become good Christians.

THURSDAY — In the spirit of being good Christians, don't shove in the line today.

FRIDAY — Try to be very courteous and helpful to your teachers today.

G) LITURGY OF THE EUCHARIST NOW TAKES PLACE:

All students who are celebrating their baptismal anniversary are asked to come and stand around the altar.

Prayer Over the Gifts

"Father, we have power to turn against you and our brothers. Help us as we offer you our gifts to always taste our need for you and one another."

Prayer After Communion

"We have broken bread and eaten, and have been nourished. Help us to go out and love others so that we may become a new creation."

SUGGESTED SONGS FOR LITURGY OF BAPTISM

"Look Beyond"

"Tell the World"

"Get Together"

"Lord, You Live"

"Into Your Hands"

"Born to Live and Die"

"New Creation"

AFTER THE LITURGY

Banner — possible quotes:
1. May all people welcome one another as brothers.
2. May you keep the candle of love burning.
3. We are one in Christ; let us love one another.
4. You're only on this earth once; you've got to give it all you've got.

Application in School

The banner should be hung in its designated place, and the posters made and changed every day.

Biblical Readings

Some suggested readings for the week:
- MONDAY — Matthew 3:13-17 and Luke 3:21,22
- TUESDAY — John 1:29-34 and 1 Corinthians 10:1,2
- WEDNESDAY — Acts 19:1-8 and Romans 5:12-20
- THURSDAY — 1 Corinthians 12:12-15
- FRIDAY — John 15:1-7

VARIATION

Epistle reading: Acts 19:2-6

NOTES:

_____
_____
_____
_____
_____
_____
_____
_____
_____
_____
_____
_____

A Liturgy for Advent

THEME

Advent is the time of the year when the Christian world prepares for the coming of the Savior. It is a time when we are called to be more open, more human. May each of us this Advent find Emmanuel, and come to know that God-is-with-us.

ORDER OF CELEBRATION

A) The celebrant enters the church as the students sing an appropriate hymn.

B) **PENITENTIAL RITE:**

    For past Advents, when we did not watch for your coming,

        LORD HAVE MERCY

    For inviting you to come to us without preparing ourselves,

        CHRIST HAVE MERCY

    For those sins which have harmed the dignity of others,

        LORD HAVE MERCY

C) **CELEBRANT READS AN APPROPRIATE PRAYER:**

    "Father, open our eyes that we may see Jesus' presence, our ears to hear his call in all events that fill our lives. Give us courage to respond, to say *yes* to carry on his work."

D) **FIRST READING:**

    We cannot touch—or even name—God-with-us
        apart from our experience of a world
            that is "charged with the grandeur of God."
    Every moment of every day
        fleshes the divine presence.

    God touches us
        in the same way that the world
            and other people
    touch us —

    Calling,
        inviting us
            to become more open,
    to become more human.

    If we answer with all we are—
        and hope to be—
            then to live
    is to live in faith
        that we have found
            and are at one with
    an incarnate God.

    The meadow is not God
        you are not God
            the patterned morning freshness
    is not God.

    But to open yourself to meadow and morning,
        to what is before you
            is to find Emmanuel, to know
    God-with-us
        as life in the moment.

                "All that came to be was alive with his life,
                and that life was the light of men."
                              (John 1:4)

        (From *Please Touch* by Edwin McMahon and
    Peter Campbell, © Sheed and Ward, Inc., 1969.)

E) **GOSPEL READING** Matthew 3:3

F) **HOMILY AND PRACTICAL ASPECTS:**
Christ is here; but we are reminded by the Church of the day Jesus "became man and dwelt among us." We prepare our lives for the occasion by renewing our baptismal commitment to lead a Christian life: We are supposed to be the voices crying out today that Jesus is still alive. To show that Jesus is still alive, we live Jesus' commandment —LOVE.

(A tall plain evergreen tree should be present in the sanctuary.)

MONDAY	— Everyone should make a "homemade" ornament to decorate the tree.
TUESDAY	— With the help of the teacher or a parent, each person should make an Advent wreath for his home.
WEDNESDAY	— Write down one positive thing that you will do to better prepare yourself for the coming of the Savior at Christmas.
THURSDAY	— If you do not have a crib set to put near the Christmas tree, ask your teacher for help in making one.
FRIDAY	— Try to show good school spirit by participating in whatever school activity you can to prepare for Christmas, like singing, or a play, etc.

G) **LITURGY OF THE EUCHARIST NOW TAKES PLACE:**

Prayer Over the Gifts

"Father, we give you bread and wine. Receive them as a sign of our love for you, and our pledge to carry out your work on earth."

Prayer After Communion

"Father we are made holy by the food of your Son. May we restore all things in you before your Son returns."

SUGGESTED SONGS FOR LITURGY OF ADVENT:

"O Come, O Come, Emmanuel"

"The Coming of Our God" (FEL-II)

"What Can a Man Say?" (FEL-II)

"Just a Closer Walk"

AFTER THE LITURGY

Banner — possible quotes:
1. The glory of God is man fully alive.
2. To seek God and (it might be) to touch and find him.
3. The light shines on in the dark.
4. God is as close to us as we can risk being close to our real selves.

Application in School
1. The banner should be hung in its designated place, and the posters made and changed every day.
2. If the celebrant feels so inclined, he could come to school during the week and help children with their Advent projects.

Biblical Readings

Some suggested readings for the week:

MONDAY — Isaiah 7:10-15
TUESDAY — Luke 1:26-38
WEDNESDAY — John 1:19-28
THURSDAY — Romans 15:4-13
FRIDAY — Isaiah 45:8

VARIATION

A Responsorial Psalm: (The Word Became Flesh and Dwelt Among Us)

The Word was more willing to become flesh than we —

(THE WORD BECAME FLESH AND DWELT AMONG US)

The Word was more willing to become life than we —

(THE WORD BECAME FLESH AND DWELT AMONG US)

The Word was more willing to become love than we —

(THE WORD BECAME FLESH AND DWELT AMONG US)

(From *Please Touch* by Edwin McMahon and Peter Campbell, © Sheed and Ward, 1969.)

Epistle reading: Isaiah 7:10-15

NOTES:

_____
_____
_____
_____
_____
_____
_____
_____
_____
_____

A Liturgy on Laws and Rules

THEME

A law is a rule made by someone in authority. Rules are for the purpose of preserving good order. Things cannot operate very well in total confusion. We will reflect today on our attitude toward rules, which are made by people who are trying to help us.

ORDER OF CELEBRATION

A) As the celebrant processes down the main aisle, the students sing an appropriate hymn.

B) **PENITENTIAL RITE:**

> For not looking at the positive side of rules,
>
> > LORD HAVE MERCY
>
> For those whose job it is to make the rules,
>
> > CHRIST HAVE MERCY
>
> For not living by the rules,
>
> > LORD HAVE MERCY

C) **CELEBRANT READS AN APPROPRIATE PRAYER:**

> "Father, they say that rules are made to have good order in a place. Help us to see rules not as a hindrance, but as an aid to understanding that true peace comes from good order."

D) **FIRST READING:**

I HATE THE RULES

I hate the rules
because, well, because they are just rules.
They are like squares on the floor,
like the circles of a target
at the rifle range,
like the lines running down the highway.

That's it,
They're like the lines on the highway,
double yellow danger lines,
and long white distance lines
and very hazy dotted lines
that vanish in the rain.

And so I've begun to wonder
about the rules
and the lines
and the rings.

What if those targets were really faces?
and what if those lines were really lives?
and what if those rules were really people?

Then sin would be breaking people
instead of breaking rules.
Sin would mean breaking up with God
instead of breaking his laws.
Sin would be personal
and cruel
and wrong. . . .

(From *For Mature Adults Only* by Norman C. Habel, Fortress Press.)

E) **GOSPEL READING:** Matthew 22:34-40

F) **HOMILY AND PRACTICAL ASPECTS:**
What would happen if no one stopped for a red light? People would get hurt. Rules, then, are really made with people in mind. Rules are for our protection. Rules help us.

Some practical aspects to be developed with the children:

MONDAY — Illustrate the results of broken rules by pictures —tragedies due to disobedience.

TUESDAY — Do what your parents say today without question.

WEDNESDAY — Point to a rule a friend is breaking that harms the good of others or himself.

THURSDAY —Make today a special day of prayer for the correct spirit of obedience to laws.

FRIDAY — Make a special effort to observe the rules that were made for the good of everyone in the classroom.

G) LITURGY OF THE EUCHARIST NOW TAKES PLACE:

Prayer Over the Gifts

"Father, we present our gifts as a sign of the rules that we live by."

Prayer After Communion

"Father, we thank you for being able to receive Communion. May we learn to live by the rules freely."

SUGGESTED SONGS FOR A LITURGY ON LAWS AND RULES:

"Jesus in Me" (John Fisher)

"Trust and Obey"

"And I Will Follow"

"Call Me by My Name, Lord"

"Shepherd's Alleluia"

AFTER THE LITURGY

Banner — possible quotes:

1. I love your law.
2. Make each day a yes day.

Application in School

The banner should be hung in its designated place, and the posters made and changed every day.

Biblical Readings

Some suggested readings for the week:

MONDAY	— Matthew 19:16-20, and 22:34-40
TUESDAY	— Matthew 5:17-48 and 19:16-19
WEDNESDAY	— Mark 12:28-34
THURSDAY	— Romans 13:8-10
FRIDAY	— James 1:25-27 and 2:12-27

VARIATION

FIRST READING: Hebrews 13:17-19

NOTES:

_____
_____
_____
_____
_____
_____
_____
_____
_____
_____

i need you!

A Liturgy on Loneliness

THEME

(Announced by students)

Today we will think of all the people who are unhappy because they are alone, and they wish they had friends. It is very sad to have no friends.

ORDER OF CELEBRATION

A) As the celebrant enters the church, an appropriate hymn is sung.

B) **PENITENTIAL RITE:**

> For those we left sad,
>> LORD HAVE MERCY
>
> For not trying to make people happy,
>> CHRIST HAVE MERCY
>
> For all the lonely people,
>> LORD HAVE MERCY

C) **CELEBRANT READS AN APPROPRIATE PRAYER:**

> "Father help us never to forget that we need you and others if we are going to make our world a better place. We ask this through Christ our Lord. Amen."

D) **FIRST READING:**

ELEANOR RIGBY

Ah, look at all the lonely people.
Ah, look at all the lonely people.

Eleanor Rigby
Picks up the rice in the church where a wedding has been,
Lives in a dream,
Waits at the window
Wearing the face that she keeps in a jar by the door.
Who is it for?

All the lonely people: Where do they all come from?
All the lonely people: Where do they all belong?

Father McKenzie
Writing the words of a sermon that no one will hear.
No one comes near.
Look at him working:
Darning his socks in the night when there's nobody there.
What does he care?

All the lonely people: Where do they all come from?
All the lonely people: Where do they all belong?

Ah, look at all the lonely people.
Ah, look at all the lonely people.

Eleanor Rigby
Died in the church and was buried along with her name.
Nobody came.
Father McKenzie
Wiping the dirt from his hands as he walks from the grave.
No one was saved.

All the lonely people: Where do they all come from?
    Ah, look at all the lonely people.
All the lonely people: Where do they all belong?
    Ah, look at all the lonely people.

(Lennon and McCartney (Beatles) © 1966
Northern Songs, Ltd., 71-75 New Oxford,
London, W.C. 1, England. By permission
of ATU Music Corp., New York.)

E) **GOSPEL READING:** Matthew 26:36-46

F) **HOMILY AND PRACTICAL ASPECTS:**

Do we really cut other people off on purpose?

People are putting their hands out to us and we ignore them.

We want to help children to see that if we deliberately ignore people the wall of loneliness will grow higher and higher.

We have to be more concerned about people. When we feel lonely we want people with us. If we don't make the effort to be with people, then, when we feel sad, no one will come to us to bring us joy.

Some practical aspects to be developed with the children during the week are:

MONDAY — During recess, if you see someone standing all alone, invite him to play with you.

TUESDAY — Bring a flower to your teacher.

WEDNESDAY — Think of the ways in which you need God. Make a visit to the church and talk to God about this.

THURSDAY — Go and visit someone in your family who lives all alone, like your grandma, your aunt, etc. Or, if they live too far, then write a letter to them. (A box will be provided in school to deposit the letters and the eighth graders will mail them.)

FRIDAY — Help those at home who need you with washing dishes, putting out the garbage, etc.

G) **LITURGY OF THE EUCHARIST NOW TAKES PLACE:**

Prayer Over the Gifts

"We need you, Father. That is why we present you these gifts — our bread and wine and ourselves."

Prayer After Communion

"This Communion shows us that we need you to nourish us in our daily life."

H) **COMMUNION MEDITATION**

After Communion everyone sits and listens to the recording (Sittin' On) "The Dock of the Bay."

SUGGESTED SONGS FOR LITURGY OF LONELINESS
  "Day Is Done"
  "Dock of the Bay"
  "All That We Have"
  "And I Will Follow"
  "My Soul Is Longing for Your Peace"
  "Keep in Mind"
  "Love Is Almost Worth the Dying"
  "Bridge Over Troubled Waters"

AFTER THE LITURGY

Banner — possible quotes:
1. To love is to risk crying.
2. Take my hand.
3. I need to be needed.
4. The question is not what we make of the Eucharist, but what the Eucharist is making of us.

Application in School
1. The banner should be hung in its designated place, and the posters made and changed every day.
2. On Thursday, the eighth-graders will pick up letters and see to it that they are mailed.

Biblical Readings

Some suggested readings for the week:

  MONDAY   — Matthew 19:16-22
  TUESDAY   — Genesis 2:18-23
  WEDNESDAY — Matthew 26:36-46
  THURSDAY — Mark 2:15-17
  FRIDAY   — James 5:13-18

VARIATION

Epistle reading: James 5:13-18

NOTES:
_____
_____
_____
_____
_____
_____
_____
_____
_____
_____
_____

A Liturgy on Choices-Decisions-Actions

THEME

All our lives we are faced with making choices, deciding, and acting upon the decisions we have made. Today we will think about the seriousness of decision-making.

ORDER OF CELEBRATION

A) Everyone is seated and listens to the recording: "Did You Ever Have to Make Up Your Mind?" (Loving Spoonful).

B) **PENITENTIAL RITE:**

    For deciding not to do our work when asked,

        LORD HAVE MERCY

    For acting before we've really decided what to do,

        CHRIST HAVE MERCY

    For choosing the easy way out,

        LORD HAVE MERCY

C) **CELEBRANT READS AN APPROPRIATE PRAYER:**

    "All-knowing Father, give us the courage to make the right decision and then to act upon it."

D) **FIRST READING:** Numbers 16:4-6

E) **GOSPEL READING:** Matthew 12:15-21

F) **HOMILY AND PRACTICAL ASPECTS:**

Some people think decision-making is a sign of maturity. Do you? Do you always think before you act? In making a decision one has to be willing to accept the consequences of his decisions. What are some of the consequences of decisions?

Some practical aspects for the week could be:

MONDAY — Look and see what has to be done to keep better order in the school, and decide to do it without being told.

TUESDAY — Offer to wash the dishes and put out the garbage.

WEDNESDAY — Offer to play with your brothers and sisters today.

THURSDAY — Offer to play with someone at school that you don't like to play with.

FRIDAY — Pray today that we always ask the Holy Spirit to guide us in making decisions.

G) **LITURGY OF THE EUCHARIST NOW TAKES PLACE:**

Prayer Over the Gifts

"Father, we have free choice to offer our gifts and ourselves to you. May we also act in the best interest of ourselves and others."

Prayer After Communion

"Father, you freely chose to give us your Son in Communion, may we live our lives according to your will."

SUGGESTED SONGS FOR LITURGY ON CHOICES — DECISIONS — ACTIONS

"Into Your Hands"

"We Need Time"

"My Soul Is Longing for Your Peace"

"And I Will Follow"

"Did You Ever Have to Make Up Your Mind?" (Loving Spoonful)

AFTER THE LITURGY

Banner — possible quotes:
1. Not to decide is to decide.
2. There is no security on this earth; there is only opportunity.
3. Experience is not what happens to you; it is what you do with what happens to you.

Application in School
The banner should be hung in its designated place and the posters changed every day.

Biblical Readings
Some suggested readings for the week:

MONDAY	— Matthew 12:38-50
TUESDAY	— Matthew 15:21-28 and Luke 6:13-15
WEDNESDAY	— Acts 1:21-26 and 1 Corinthians 1:27-28
THURSDAY	— Luke 5:10-11 and 27-28
FRIDAY	— Luke 18:22-30

NOTES:

_____
_____
_____
_____
_____
_____
_____
_____
_____

A Liturgy on Self-Awareness

THEME

Often we imitate other people instead of being ourselves — the kind of persons God really meant us to be. Today we want to spend some time thinking about ourselves as persons — not imitations.

ORDER OF CELEBRATION

A) The celebrant processes down the aisle while the students sing an appropriate song.

B) **PENITENTIAL RITE:**

    For not realizing "I am what I am,"

        LORD HAVE MERCY

    For forgetting at times that others are persons,

        CHRIST HAVE MERCY

    For forgetting sometimes that God is for real,

        LORD HAVE MERCY

C) **CELEBRANT READS AN APPROPRIATE PRAYER:**

    "Father, guess what, I am great, I am a person, your child. May I better understand what all this means."

D) **FIRST READING:** Exodus 3:13-15

E) **GOSPEL READING:** John 1:19-23

F) **HOMILY AND PRACTICAL ASPECTS:**

Why do people imitate people? If you spend all your time imitating other people, then you don't get to know who you really are.

More time should be spent doing the things that we can do well instead of trying to do things the way other people do them.

Some practical applications of the liturgy may be:

MONDAY — Try putting a patch on your eye and see how it feels to be blind even in one eye.

TUESDAY — Write down the ways in which you have imitated others instead of being yourself—especially the times you try to imitate the people you like.

WEDNESDAY — Try to be very good in the cafeteria today.

THURSDAY — Pray today that you could come to understand a little better who you really are, and all the good things God has done for you.

FRIDAY — Try to remember who your teacher is and the job that teachers have to do. Be kind to them.

G) **LITURGY OF THE EUCHARIST NOW TAKES PLACE:**

Prayer Over the Gifts

"Father, accept these gifts of bread and wine, signs of our total giving. Help us to realize the statement: 'I am what I am.'"

Prayer After Communion

"Father we thank you for giving us Jesus in Communion, may he help us never to forget that we are persons and that other people are also."

SUGGESTED SONGS FOR LITURGY ON SELF-AWARENESS:

"Gonna Sing My Lord"

"Of My Hands"

"Man of Mind"

"Take Our Bread"

"Sing Praise to the Lord"
"Sing Out His Goodness"
"We Need Time"

AFTER THE LITURGY

Banner — possible quotes:

1. The Glory of God is man fully alive.
2. God is as close to us as we can risk being close to our real selves.

Application in School

The banner should be hung in its designated place and the posters changed every day.

Biblical Readings

Some suggested readings for the week:

MONDAY — Matthew 18:21-22 and Matthew 22:34-40
TUESDAY — Luke 10:25-28 and Mark 12:28-31
WEDNESDAY — 1 John 4:17-21 and 1 John 3:14-17
THURSDAY — Romans 15:5-7 and Ephesians 6:1-7
FRIDAY — Matthew 23:15 and John 20:21-23

NOTES:

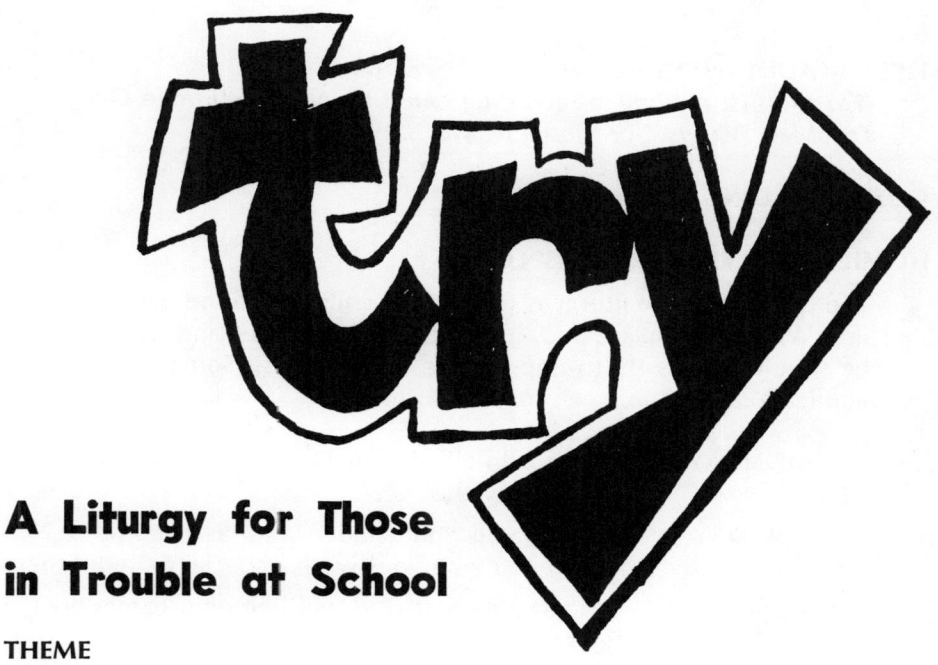

A Liturgy for Those in Trouble at School

THEME

Today we would like to think about those students who are grateful for being able to have so many opportunities at school, but who find learning very hard or uninteresting.

ORDER OF CELEBRATION

A) The celebrant processes into the church while students sing an appropriate song.

B) **PENITENTIAL RITE:**

    For giving up when we don't understand our studies,

        LORD HAVE MERCY

    For not looking for help from our teachers or fellow classmates,

        CHRIST HAVE MERCY

    For forgetting to call upon God when times get rough,

        LORD HAVE MERCY

C) **CELEBRANT READS AN APPROPRIATE PRAYER:**

    "Father, it is great that we have so much to learn, but it doesn't come easy for all of us. Help us, when we have difficulties, not to give up."

D) **FIRST READING:**
(For the first reading, a recording could be played, "Bridge Over Troubled Waters," or "Jesus in Me" by John Fisher.)

E) **GOSPEL READING:** Luke 7:11-15

F) **HOMILY AND PRACTICAL ASPECTS:**
The purpose of the liturgy is to help the child realize he never gives up. With the help of God, his teachers, classmates and parents, he should always try to improve his study habits. Some practical applications for the week may be as follows:

MONDAY	— Try to do all of your homework or classwork every day this week.
TUESDAY	— When you don't understand, ask people to help you with your work, especially the teacher.
WEDNESDAY	— Pray today that God will help you to understand your schoolwork.
THURSDAY	— Try to make a schedule in which you have time to study without the television, or try to schedule some reading time.
FRIDAY	— Let your parents see your test papers, even the bad ones, so they will know what you are doing in school.

G) **LITURGY OF THE EUCHARIST NOW TAKES PLACE:**

Prayer Over the Gifts

"Father, present at your altar are bread and wine, signs of our trust in you. Help us when our studies get difficult."

Prayer After Communion

"Father, by partaking in this Eucharist, give us a closer sharing in your wisdom. May you be a sign of never giving up."

SUGGESTED SONGS FOR LITURGY FOR THOSE IN TROUBLE AT SCHOOL:

"My Soul Is Longing for Your Peace"

"All That We Have"

"Keep in Mind"

"Of My Hands"

"The Spirit of the Lord"

"Jesus in Me" — John Fisher
"Love Is Almost Worth the Dying"

AFTER THE LITURGY

Banner — possible quotes:
1. To seek God and (it might be) to touch and find him.
2. I get by with a little help from my friends.

Application in School
The banner should be hung in its designated place, and the posters changed every day.

Biblical Readings
Some suggested readings for the week:

MONDAY — Job 1:12-22
TUESDAY — Job 2:7-10
WEDNESDAY — Job 5:7-11
THURSDAY — Psalm 22
FRIDAY — Psalm 25

VARIATION
First Reading: Acts 3:1-10

NOTES:

A Liturgy on Creation

THEME

Creation means making something out of nothing. Of all the things that God created, man is the greatest. Today we will celebrate a liturgy of God's creation, especially the creation of our friends.

ORDER OF CELEBRATION

A) The celebrant does not process up the main aisle, but rather is seated in the presidential chair for the entrance reading.

Friends

Did you ever feel — Oh, I don't know, just OUT OF IT?
Separate, disconnected, an outsider to everything?
Vance did, and Vance was no dummy.
He was a sharp San Antonio kid, played football, went dancing, had a job, got good grades — just knew the score.
But just now down deep he felt very much out of it.
He was walking down Commerce, buses rumbling and cars rolling at his side—people, stores, newsstands all around.
Signs on the windows: "Sale: Buy now; don't miss it!"
A million magazines sold by old men all the same — promising hot sex, cool love like a meat market.
Everyone he saw was behind a kind of window and he was on the outside trying to look in.
It felt terrible.

How was it possible to stand in the middle of crowds, stores, signs, and feel so ALONE?
It was weird, really bad news! Feeling like you are stuck in a desert, or stranded on an island while your feet pound pavement and people's elbows and packages and shoulders bang against you.

Vance stood on a corner: hurry up and change red light, thinking about windows and deserts, islands and feeling alone.
He thought about that poem — last semester in English.
The one about, ". . . no man is an island. . ."
That feeling, that sense of aloneness Vance and so many feel at times — they all mean the same:
I'M LOST, GOD, SO LOST.

(Reprinted with permission from *Don't Just Stand There!* by Earnest Larsen, C.SS.R. A Liguorian Book, © 1969 Liguorian Books, Liguori, Mo. 63057.)

(Students are now asked to stand arm in arm for the singing of the Hymn — "No Man Is an Island.")

B) **PENITENTIAL RITE:**

For being angry and deliberately trying to hurt others who are also my friends,

LORD HAVE MERCY

For being jealous of others and ungrateful for the many gifts you have given each of us,

CHRIST HAVE MERCY

For not going out of our way to help others because we might be hurt or because it's too much trouble,

LORD HAVE MERCY

C) **CELEBRANT READS AN APPROPRIATE PRAYER:**

"Our Father, from whom we came and to whom we return, help us never to cease to answer your call to friendship with you and one another."

D) **FIRST READING:**

WHY MAN WAS CREATED

Hunger is my native place in the land of the passions.

Hunger for fellowship, hunger for righteousness — for a fellowship founded on righteousness, and a righteousness attained in fellowship.

Only life can satisfy the demands of life. And this hunger of mine can be satisfied for the simple reason that the nature of life is such that I can realize my individuality by becoming a bridge for others, a stone in the temple of righteousness.

Don't be afraid of yourself, live your individuality to the full — but for the good of others. Don't copy others in order to buy fellowship, or make convention your law instead of living the righteousness.

To become free and responsible. For this alone was man created, and he who fails to take the Way which could have been his shall be lost eternally.

>   (From *Markings,* by Dag Hammarskjold, translated by Leif Sjoberg and W. H. Auden. Copyright © 1964 by Alfred A. Knopf, Inc. and Faber & Faber Ltd. Reprinted by permission of the publisher.)

E) **GOSPEL READING:** Luke 11:5-8

F) **HOMILY AND PRACTICAL ASPECTS:**

There should be a dialogue homily with the children on the aspects of creation — God's gifts to us. This liturgy is to help us realize that all things created are important, good and beautiful. We too can participate in God's creative act through friendship — we can create friendships; people should be the greatest active concern of our lives. Some practical applications for the week may be as follows:

MONDAY	— Draw or make some things that God created, and on Thursday display your work on the bulletin board or the display table.
TUESDAY	— Bring to your teacher an unusual thing from God's creation.
WEDNESDAY	— Let someone know how happy you are to have him for a friend by sharing something with him or helping him in his schoolwork.
THURSDAY	— Write, with the help of your teacher, the meaning you get out of the song: "Come Along to the New Creation."
FRIDAY	— Help make something in the kitchen.

G) LITURGY OF THE EUCHARIST NOW TAKES PLACE:

Prayer Over the Gifts

"Father, these gifts are the work of your hands which you have given us. Accept them as we gather around your table in friendship."

Prayer After Communion

"Father, we thank you for the gift of your Son, who deepens us in love. May our lips now speak peace to all men; may the works of our hands and mind awaken all lives to new life in Jesus."

SUGGESTED SONGS FOR LITURGY OF CREATION

"The New Creation"

"Let All the Earth"

"Turn Your Eyes"

"All of My Life"

"And I Will Follow"

"Kill I Never Will" (FEL-II)

"Friends"

"Day Is Done"

"No Man Is an Island"

AFTER THE LITURGY

Banner — possible quotes:

1. No man is an island.
2. Every individual is a miracle.
3. Welcome, to the new creation.
4. You are my miracle.
5. I need you.

Application in School

1. The banner should be hung in its designated place, and the posters made and changed every day.
2. On Friday, the celebrant should visit the display the children made on creation in each classroom.

Biblical Readings

Some suggested readings for the week:
- MONDAY — 1 Corinthians 15:45-58
- TUESDAY — 2 Corinthians 5:17
- WEDNESDAY — Romans 8:18-22
- THURSDAY — James 1:18
- FRIDAY — Matthew 8:23-27 and 10:34-36

VARIATIONS

First Reading: Genesis 1:26-27
Gospel Reading: John 15:12-17

NOTES:

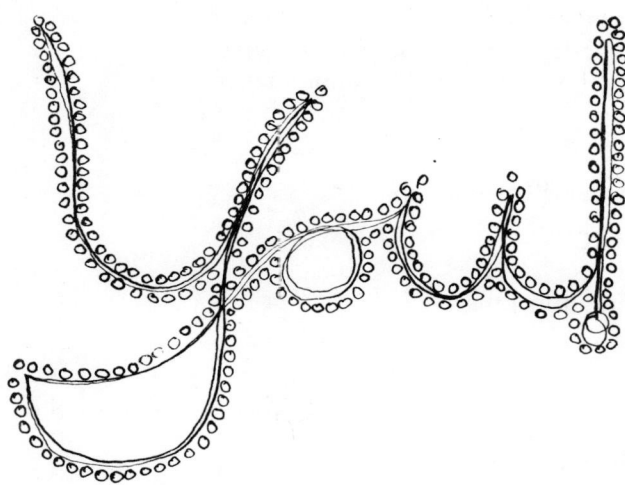

A Liturgy on Love

THEME

Love has many voices. Love sends its greeting in the smile of a friend, the contented sighs of a baby, the felt whisperings of the Spirit.

Often we are slow to recognize how many voices are really love's voice.

"God is love," says John the Evangelist. "He who dwells in love is dwelling in God, and God in him."

Love speaks in many places. It leans against the neighbor's fence or comes sniffing into a kitchen filled with cooking. It walks amid the bustle of the city streets or stands on a crowded bus.

Love has many moods. Sometimes love is bold and happy, and sometimes it is anxious and hesitant. Sometimes it is riotous and demanding, or gentle and relaxed, or even sober and practical. Sometimes love just waits.

Love comes in all seasons. It rides the icy winds of winter and laughs with raindrops in the spring. It wanders through the restless heat of summer and catches leaves of autumn as they fall.

Listen to love.

> (*Listen to Love*, edited by Louis M. Savary, S.J. Published by The Regina Press, Hicksville, N.Y. 11801. 1970.)

A) **ORDER OF CELEBRATION**

As soon as someone is through reading the theme, a recording is played. Any recording that would recapture the above-mentioned theme would be suitable. This is followed by a meditative pause.

B) **PENITENTIAL RITE:**

For not having loved ourselves enough,
> LORD HAVE MERCY

For having loved others too little,
> CHRIST HAVE MERCY

For not having recognized that what the world needs most is love,
> LORD HAVE MERCY

C) **CELEBRANT READS AN APPROPRIATE PRAYER:**

"Father, we are not alone, we need to love. Help us to forget ourselves for others, so that in giving ourselves, we may teach ourselves to love."

D) **FIRST READING:**

LOVE

Love is for freedom, and freedom is for love. When love beckons you, follow him, for that which you follow is pure freedom —Christ (mystery of love).

To understand Christ is to face freedom — for Christ lived to make us aware of freedom. When freedom is present, Christ can be felt, for it is then when the spirit in the depth of our being cries to be free from the self. It cries to be free, because it is the self which tries to hold this spirit from being free. It is the Spirit of Christ in individuals who cry to be freed and to be united in the bond of pure love, but it is our selfishness and fear to understand our Creator which do not allow our spirits to unite in love.

I cry to share my uniqueness with you, because the Christ in me desires to know the Christ in you. I ask you only one thing —when will you free Christ from yourself and become a member in the Heart of Christ?

My humanity and the depth of spirit within me must be united with that spirit within you so that I may become human.

Love is like life, for just as life has trials, so does love.

I now ask that you become a man with me. For without you, and you without me, manhood is lost for both of us.
(Andrew Joffrion)

E) **GOSPEL READING:** John 13:33-35

F) **HOMILY AND PRACTICAL APPLICATIONS:**

The reading of the epistle lends itself to good dialogue with the children. Some practical applications for this week's liturgy are:

MONDAY	— Share your toys with your brothers and sisters or friends that come over to play.
TUESDAY	— Be kind to the other students in school today.
WEDNESDAY	— Discuss with your teacher the corporal works of mercy.
THURSDAY	— Do something for mom and dad today that would show them you really love them. It would be even better if you told them that before you go to bed.
FRIDAY	— Let today be a special day of prayer, that we may learn to love God and our neighbor as we are called to love.

G) **LITURGY OF THE EUCHARIST NOW TAKES PLACE:**

Prayer Over the Gifts

"Father, we give you these gifts of bread and wine. They are signs of our love for you."

Prayer After Communion

"Father, by sharing at your table with the one we love may we go forth to share this love with others."

SUGGESTED SONGS FOR LITURGY ON LOVE:

"Love, Love"

"I'll Never Fall in Love Again"

"That's No Way to Say Good-bye"

"Love Is Almost Worth the Dying"

"Love One Another"

"Man of Mind"

"Shepherd's Alleluia"

AFTER THE LITURGY

Banner — possible quotes:
1. To love is to risk crying.
2. The day you no longer burn with love, many others will die of the cold.

Application in School

The banner should be hung in its designated place, and the posters changed every day.

Biblical Readings

Some suggested readings for the week:

MONDAY	— Matthew 27:39-44 and Acts 2:23-26
TUESDAY	— John 17: 23-26 and John 3:16-17
WEDNESDAY	— Matthew 20:1-16 and Romans 8:14-17
THURSDAY	— Luke 10:1-12
FRIDAY	— John 10:1-12

Due to the length of the selections quoted — portions of these readings may be read either at general assemblies or in the classroom during the week or they may be made into a responsorial psalm after the readings.

VARIATION

Epistle reading: I Corinthians 13:1-7

NOTES:

A Liturgy on Death

THEME

"There is a time to be born, and a time to die." Today we will think about death and how it separates us for a time from the people we love.

ORDER OF CELEBRATION

A) The celebrant processess into the church while students sing an appropriate song.

B) **PENITENTIAL RITE:**

    For preservation from final death which separates us from what we love most,

        LORD HAVE MERCY

    For all those who have died so we may live,

        CHRIST HAVE MERCY

    For our lack of understanding of death,

        LORD HAVE MERCY

C) **CELEBRANT READS AN APPROPRIATE PRAYER:**

    "Father, we come before you, questioning and uncertain. Help us understand why in your good time you call people back into your hands."

D) **FIRST READING:**

"Death"

People were following:
    The family—some crying,
        Some pretending to cry;
    Friends—some grieving,
        Some bored or chatting.

Leaving the cemetery, some of the family were sobbing: "All is finished." Others were sniffling: "Come, come, my dear, courage: it's finished." Some friends murmured: "Poor man, that's how we'll all finish." And I was thinking that everything was just beginning.

As if there were dead people. There are no dead people, Lord. There are only the living, on earth and beyond. Death exists, Lord, but it's nothing but a moment, a second, a step, the step from provisional to permanent, from temporal to eternal, as in the death of the child the adolescent is born, from the caterpillar emerges the butterfly, from the grain the full-blown sheath.

Life is going to last, Life is eternal.

("The Funeral." From *Prayers* by Michel Quoist,
© Sheed and Ward, Inc., 1963.)

E) **GOSPEL READING:** John 11:17-26

F) **HOMILY AND PRACTICAL ASPECTS:**
    Death is something we all experience. Death should be a sign for us to *live*. Experiencing the death of a friend or relative should give us more encouragement and more willingness to give ourselves to other people. Death is a time to evaluate our lives and all the opportunities that are presented to us to live as Christians and give ourselves to others.

Some practical applications for this week's liturgy are the following:

    MONDAY   — Wear the butterflies that we will receive at the celebration to school during the rest of the week.

    TUESDAY   — Ask your parents to tell you all about what your grandparents (or any other relative) were like before they died.

    WEDNESDAY — Make a booklet of magazine pictures on "What death means to me."

    THURSDAY   — See if there is anything you as a Christian can do to make another person really alive.

    FRIDAY   — Pray today in a special way, asking God to help you accept "the mystery of death," and to be a fully *alive* Christian while you are living.

G) LITURGY OF THE EUCHARIST NOW TAKES PLACE:

(During this time all students could come forward at Offertory time and pick up a butterfly made of felt and wear it. This could serve as a symbol of the death-resurrection reality for the child.)

Prayer Over the Gifts

"Father, we offer you our gifts and prayers. Help us to know that death and darkness are not the end. The cocoon becomes a butterfly!"

Prayer After Communion

"Father, we have shared bread around your table. Reassure us that those you have taken to yourself are still close to us."

SUGGESTED SONGS FOR LITURGY ON DEATH:

"I Am the Resurrection"
"I Am the Bread of Life"
"All My Trials"
"Love Is Almost Worth the Dying"
"Into Your Hands"
"Sing Praise to the Lord"
"Born to Live and Die"

AFTER THE LITURGY

Banner — possible quote:

The light shines on in the dark.

Application in School

1. The banner should be hung in its designated place, and the posters changed every day.
2. On Friday the celebrant may want to visit the rooms and see the booklets.

Biblical Readings

Some suggestions for the week:

MONDAY — John 11:32-38

TUESDAY — 1 Corinthians 15:25-28
WEDNESDAY — Luke 10:25-28
THURSDAY — Mark 9:43-48
FRIDAY — Matthew 7:13,14 and 22:23-33

VARIATION

FIRST READING: Revelation 21:1-5

NOTES:

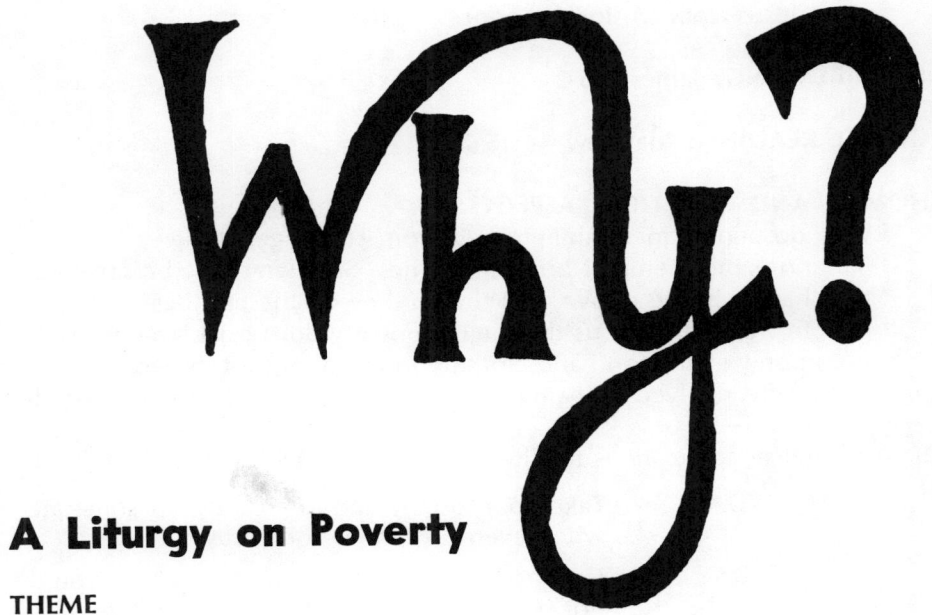

A Liturgy on Poverty

THEME

"Blessed are the poor in spirit, for theirs is the kingdom of heaven." Sometimes we define poverty as the condition of those who have not the food, clothing, shelter and recreation necessary to keep up with the normal standard of living. Many people are poor through their own fault. However, the conditions of our society are responsible for the many poor and oppressed in our country today. We wish to think about the many poor people that we continue to oppress and ignore.

ORDER OF CELEBRATION
A) The celebrant processes into the church while students sing an appropriate song.

B) **PENITENTIAL RITE:**

You have come to enrich the poor,

> LORD HAVE MERCY

For our complacency under the pressure of great poverty,

> CHRIST HAVE MERCY

For our refusal to do anything for the oppressed,

> LORD HAVE MERCY

C) **CELEBRANT READS AN APPROPRIATE PRAYER:**

"Father, may we be converted from our complacency and learn to share Jesus' concern for the poor."

D) **FIRST READING:** James 2:5-9

E) **GOSPEL READING:** Matthew 14:15-21

F) **HOMILY AND PRACTICAL ASPECTS:**
Why do people in Washington, Detroit, Los Angeles, Newark, Baltimore and Memphis burn their cities? Shouldn't they be satisfied they have a house to live in? Why do they do these things? These people want to show us that unjust poverty does exist. The answer is not in only giving food and clothing to the poor, but in becoming personally involved in seeing that they become treated as real people.

Some practical applications for this week's liturgy are:

MONDAY	— Take your money and buy candy for someone who never has money for candy.
TUESDAY	— Go through your clothes and bring what you do not need or does not fit you to the clothes drive for the poor.
WEDNESDAY	— Help students who do poorly in their schoolwork.
THURSDAY	— Today a special collection will be picked up and sent to the poor in any foreign country that the students vote on.
FRIDAY	— Today special prayers will be said in the classroom that we may be moved by the Holy Spirit to become more conscious in our lives of the needs of the poor.

G) **LITURGY OF THE EUCHARIST NOW TAKES PLACE:**

Prayer Over the Gifts

"Father, you know we have failed, and let down those who suffer. As we present our gifts to you, give us your Spirit so that we can do something for the poor."

Prayer After Communion

"Father, having received Communion we pray that we may cooperate with Jesus in his work on earth and in his concern for the poor."

SUGGESTED SONGS FOR LITURGY ON POVERTY:

"Whatsoever You Do"

"Sign of Total Giving"

"Come, Let Us Go"

"Man of Mind"

"Get Together"

"We Shall Overcome"

"Come in, Pilgrim"

"Have You Ever Been"

(Any popular recording on poverty and related social problems.)

AFTER THE LITURGY

Banner — possible quotes:

1. Smile on your brother.
2. The greatest good we can do for others is not just to share our riches with them, but to reveal their riches to themselves.
3. If a free society cannot help the many who are poor, it cannot save the few who are rich.

Application in School

1. The banner should be hung in its designated place, and the posters changed every day.
2. On Tuesday, boxes should be provided for the clothes drive and means provided for distributing the clothes to the poor.
3. On Thursday an eighth grade student could pick up the school's collection for the poor and the voting results on the name of the country should be made known to the entire student body.

Biblical Readings

Some suggested readings for the week:

MONDAY — Luke 2:1-20 and 4:16-20

TUESDAY — Luke 6:20-26 and Matthew 11:2-6

WEDNESDAY — Matthew 11:25-27 and 11:28-29

THURSDAY — Matthew 25:31-46 and John 10:11-17

FRIDAY — John 13:1-8 and 19:34-36

NOTES:

Give out "Smile" buttons.

A Liturgy on Values

THEME

The theme for our celebration is value. Today would be a good day to examine ourselves and see what we think is important in our lives.

ORDER OF CELEBRATION

A) The celebrant enters the church, while an appropriate hymn is sung.

B) **PENITENTIAL RITE:**

> For having false values that only bring misery rather than peace,
>
> > LORD HAVE MERCY
>
> For the many times when we have made wealth and material possession into small gods,
>
> > CHRIST HAVE MERCY
>
> Your mercy liberates us from false values and empty goals,
>
> > LORD HAVE MERCY

C) **CELEBRANT READS AN APPROPRIATE PRAYER:**

> "Father, help us to see that all the things you have made have value."

D) **FIRST READING:**

E) **GOSPEL READING:** Matthew 25:14-30

F) **HOMILY AND PRACTICAL ASPECTS:**
Material goods do have value, but today we are stressing the value of honesty, goodness, beauty, justice, etc., in the life of a child.

If available, a film from a value series could be shown. If not, we recommend some technique from *Values and Teachings,* by Raths, Harmin, and Simon. Merrill Publishing Co., 1966.

Some practical suggestions for the week may be as follows:

MONDAY — Make a scrapbook, showing on the same page the positive and negative aspects of some things we value.

TUESDAY — With the aid of the teacher, we could review value indicators such as (1) goals or purposes (2) aspirations (3) attitudes (4) interests (5) feelings (6) beliefs (7) activities (8) worries, problems, and obstacles.

WEDNESDAY — Do some role playing in the class.

THURSDAY — Discuss how God fits into our value world.

FRIDAY — Talk with your parents today about the work you have done this week on value.

G) **LITURGY OF THE EUCHARIST NOW TAKES PLACE:**

Prayer Over the Gifts

"Father, this bread and wine we offer you show the work of man's hand. May they help us to see the value of your work."

Prayer After Communion

"Father, now that we have received your Son in Communion, may we come to see the value of other people."

SUGGESTED SONGS FOR LITURGY ON VALUES:

"All That We Have"

"All Our Joy"

"Less of Me"

"Sign of Total Giving"

"Born to Live and Die"

AFTER THE LITURGY

Banner — possible quotes:
1. How glorious it is and also how painful to be an exception.
2. Great minds discuss ideas, average minds discuss events, small minds discuss people.

Application in School
1. The banner should be hung in its designated place, and the posters made and changed every day.
2. The celebrant should visit the classrooms and look at the scrapbooks the students made.

Biblical Readings
Some suggested readings for the week:

MONDAY	— Matthew 10:9-10 and Luke 10:4-8
TUESDAY	— Romans 15:25-32 and 1 Corinthians 16:1-4
WEDNESDAY	— Matthew 6:19-21 and Mark 10:29-30
THURSDAY	— Luke 12:33-34
FRIDAY	— Luke 16:1-13 and 19-31

VARIATION

Epistle reading: Acts 5:1-11

VALUE

We do not come to believe in ourselves until someone
reveals that deep inside us
something is valuable,
worth listening to
worthy of our trust
sacred to our touch.

(From *Please Touch* by Edwin McMahon and Peter Campbell. © Sheed and Ward, Inc., 1969.)

NOTES:

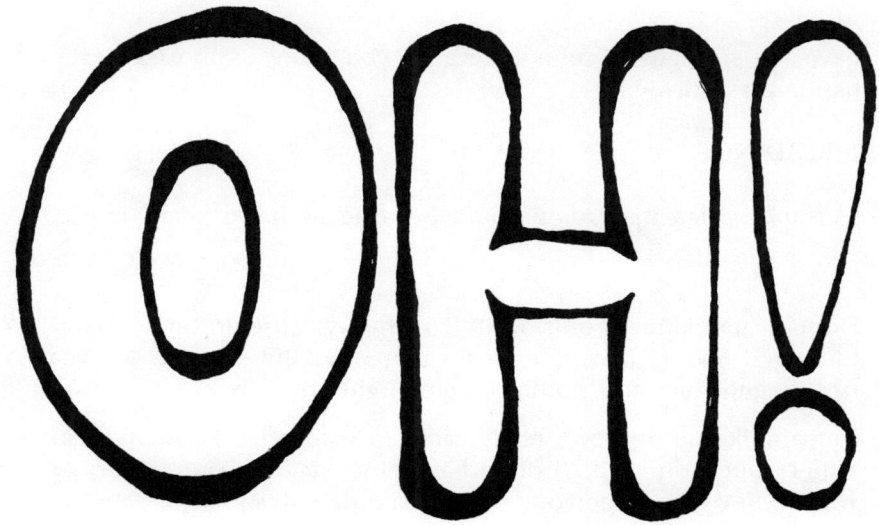

A Liturgy for Those Tempted by Drugs

THEME

Jesus Christ holds the only key to the solution to any basic human problem. Jesus can change the lives of people. God can help us to be renewed without the use of pills or drugs. Today we want to pray for all people, especially young ones, who use drugs as a cop-out.

ORDER OF CELEBRATION

A) The celebrant enters the church while the students sing an appropriate hymn.

B) **PENITENTIAL RITE:**

For all children who push drugs,

> LORD HAVE MERCY

For all children who are taking drugs,

> CHRIST HAVE MERCY

That we search for happiness with people and not drugs,

> LORD HAVE MERCY

C) **CELEBRANT READS AN APPROPRIATE PRAYER:**

"Father, there are pushers and those drawn to drugs. Help us to have the strength to refuse, because you bring us the greatest happiness and joy."

D) **FIRST READING:**

(An appropriate recording could be used as background music.)

STONED

Stoned. Just kind of outside it. Not heavy. Just drifting. That's the way I like it. It wasn't always that way. But 16, now 18, years of this and that, and nothing seems right anymore.

I mean, like no one ever really cared or wanted to know me. Sure I tried, but mom said, "I don't have time, stay out of my hair, go watch television, wipe your nose." And dad always said, "Not now, I'm busy, have to catch a plane, make a deal, write a book, propose a research." At school they never did want to know me or us. They want us to read a book, do mathematics, know research, decline a verb.

At church they never did see me. They wanted us not to listen to *that* music, not do this, that, or anything else, and there's no love.

And war is there when we get out. And people die. And the human race fouls its nest. So I want out. Don't hassle me. I won't belong. What: Is there love? A real peace movement? Show them where our heads are? Together? Stop the war? No more kids killed? Wow! Kill the pigs? Burn it down? Pick up the gun? Stoned. Just kind of outside it. Not heavy. Just drifting. That's the way I like it.

No, God, you're not real and neither is love. What? You care? So show it! You sent your Son? I can be a member of your family? Forever? How? Ask Jesus into my life? Too weird. Too simple. Okay, I'll try it. Come on in, Jesus, and be my real friend.

(From *The Street People,* by the *Right On!* staff, the American Baptist Board of Education and Publication, Valley Forge, Pa. 1971. Used by permission.)

E) **RESPONSORIAL:**
Listen to the recording, "He Was a Most Peculiar Man," by Simon and Garfunkel, Charing Cross Music Inc. 1965.

F) **GOSPEL READING:** John 14:1-4

G) **HOMILY AND PRACTICAL ASPECTS:**

Too often, the negative aspects of drugs — "the law," "don't get caught, you'll end up in jail" or "it may be harmful to the body and mind," "the experiences are sometimes bad" — are stressed as a very good reason for not taking drugs. But, drugs are a cop-out, not an answer. The only answer is Jesus. He helps us to face the reality of the problems in our lives.

MONDAY — Collect pictures of drug addicts and drugs for display on the bulletin board.

TUESDAY — Help your parents today with the dishes, or garbage or supper.

WEDNESDAY — Say special prayers today for all students, that they may not turn to drugs as a cop-out.

THURSDAY — Write a paper on why a teenager *should not* want to use drugs.

FRIDAY — Discuss your paper in class today with other students.

H) **LITURGY OF THE EUCHARIST NOW TAKES PLACE:**

Prayer Over the Gifts

"Father, we offer you bread and wine, grant that we choose what is best for us."

Prayer After Communion

"Father, we have broken bread together, may this union with Jesus and each other free us from looking for other means of finding happiness."

SUGGESTED SONGS FOR THE LITURGY FOR THOSE TEMPTED BY DRUGS:

"Fire and Rain" (James Taylor)

"Man of Mind"

"We Need Time"

"All That We Have"

"My Sweet Lord"

"My Soul Is Longing for Your Peace"

AFTER THE LITURGY

Banner — possible quotes:

1. Pray that your loneliness may spur you into finding something

to live for.

2. She slumps against the window, passive, limp, lifeless, but within, how she screams. How she begs, soul outstretched, for sanctuary.

Application in School

The banner should be hung in its designated place, and the posters made and changed every day.

Biblical Readings

Some suggested readings for the week:

MONDAY — Matthew 4:1-11 and Mark 1:12-13
TUESDAY — Luke 4:1-13 and Matthew 26:36-46
WEDNESDAY — Matthew 16:21-23
THURSDAY — James 1:2-3
FRIDAY — 1 Peter 1:6-7

VARIATION

First Reading: 1 Peter 1:6-9

NOTES:

_____
_____
_____
_____
_____
_____
_____
_____

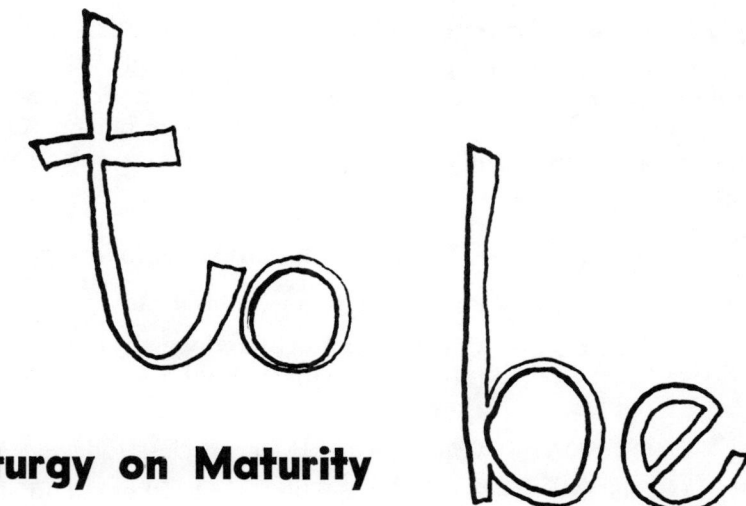

A Liturgy on Maturity

THEME

Each of us has to grow, to develop as persons — to mature — in mind and body. Let us think today about this growth process, our maturing.

ORDER OF CELEBRATION

A) The celebrant enters down the main aisle. An appropriate hymn is sung.

B) **PENITENTIAL RITE:**

> That we understand that every single muscle in our body plays an important part in our growth,
>
> > LORD HAVE MERCY
>
> For the times we refused to let others help us grow,
>
> > CHRIST HAVE MERCY
>
> For not growing in the love of God,
>
> > LORD HAVE MERCY

C) **CELEBRANT READS AN APPROPRIATE PRAYER:**

> "Father, you who share life with us in our sharing of life with others, may you touch us with your Spirit and nourish our growth."

D) **FIRST READING:** 2 Peter 3:13-18

E) **GOSPEL READING:** Mark 4:26-29

F) **HOMILY AND PRACTICAL ASPECTS:**
We are all aware of our physical and mental growth. As we grow, and get older, we also hope that we are maturing. For a person really to "grow," he must be touched by another person. Only by the encouragement and assistance of others does a person really grow.

Some practical applications for the week may be as follows:

MONDAY	— Plant a seed and watch it grow.
TUESDAY	— Check your height and weight today and mark it down on paper; about a month from now, check it again.
WEDNESDAY	— Volunteer to answer in class today.
THURSDAY	— Play a game with your brother(s) and sister(s).
FRIDAY	— Say some special prayers today that God will help you mature gracefully.

G) **LITURGY OF THE EUCHARIST NOW TAKES PLACE:**

Prayer Over the Gifts

"Father, as we offer ourselves to you this day, help us to be willing to take the risk of the uncertainties of love rather than remain locked in loneliness."

Prayer After Communion

"Father, having broken bread together, pour out your Spirit upon us and make us strong in love, alive with concern, warm with gentle strength, and openhearted in sharing."

RECESSIONAL:
The celebrant can distribute seeds to all the students as they leave the church building.

SUGGESTED SONGS FOR LITURGY ON MATURING:

"Sign of Total Giving"

"Heal Your People"

"Born to Live and Die"

"Look All Around" (FEL-II)
"Day Is Done"
"Road of Life" (FEL-II)

AFTER THE LITURGY

Banner — possible quotes:

1. What I am to be, I am becoming.
2. In loving, we discover more about ourselves.
3. To love scmeone is to invite him to grow.

Application in School

The banner should be hung in its designated place, and the posters made and changed every day.

Biblical Readings

Some suggested readings for the week:

MONDAY	— Matthew 13:24-30
TUESDAY	— Luke 8:4-8
WEDNESDAY	— 2 Peter 3:13-18
THURSDAY	— Mark 4: 26-29
FRIDAY	— 2 Thessalonians 1:3-6

NOTES:

_____

_____

_____

_____

_____

_____

_____

A Liturgy on Thanksgiving

THEME

The Book of Proverbs says, "Honor the Lord with substance, and the first fruits of all your increase. So shall your barns be filled with plenty, and your presses shall burst out with new wine." Let us on this Thanksgiving Day honor the Lord with substance.

ORDER OF CELEBRATION

A) The celebrant processes down the main aisle of the church, the servers may carry a small arrangement of fruit and wheat and place this near or on the altar. An appropriate entrance hymn is sung.

B) **PENITENTIAL RITE:**

> For allowing our brothers and sisters to go hungry,
>
> > LORD HAVE MERCY
>
> For not giving you thanks for each other,
>
> > CHRIST HAVE MERCY
>
> For not sharing what you give us,
>
> > LORD HAVE MERCY

C) **CELEBRANT READS AN APPROPRIATE PRAYER:**

"We gather here, Father, to thank you for the wonders of your world; May we never forget what you give us. We ask through Christ our Lord, Amen."

D) **FIRST READING:**

THANKSGIVING AGAIN

The Day has come — a nation pauses, Lord,
To thank Thee for the blessing of the year.
Great have been Thy mercies, and reward
Despite mankind's strange faltering and fear;
Our lack of trust when dark drought stalked the land,
Our lack of faith when dangers threatened sore,
And all the while from Thy great outflung hand
The harvest came, a bright abundant store.

Out of the past, a voice: "We shall set aside
A day to thank the Giver of all good."
From a colony to a continent spreading wide
That voice still rings, and we, too, as we should,
Give thanks to Thee, Lord God, with sincere praise,
For Thy mercies that surround us through our days.

(From *Let the Sun Shine In* by Grace Noll Crowell. Copyrighted © 1970 by Fleming H. Revell Co. Used by permission.)

E) **RESPONSORIAL: THANK YOU, LORD, THANK YOU**

1) Thank you for the sky, dawn, sunset, the sun, moon, the stars

    THANK YOU, LORD, THANK YOU

2) Thank you for water, trees, mountains, the levee, hills, fields, grass, flowers, soil

    THANK YOU, LORD, THANK YOU

3) Thank you for our dog, cat, the chickens and ducks, the canary, the horses and cows

    THANK YOU, LORD, THANK YOU

4) Thank you for our toys, comic books, toothbrush and toothpaste, soap, towels, shoes, clothes, for our house, for my radio

    THANK YOU, LORD, THANK YOU

5) Thank you for mother and dad, for sister and brother, for our teachers, for my friend down the street, for my grandparents

   THANK YOU, LORD, THANK YOU

6) Thank you for the smiling faces; the crying faces; helping hands; dirty feet, strong muscles, singing voices

   THANK YOU, LORD, THANK YOU

F) **GOSPEL READING:** Matthew 15:32-39

G) **HOMILY AND PRACTICAL ASPECTS:**
Perhaps everyone could share together the story of the first Thanksgiving and all the things that we want to thank God for, especially each other.

Some practical applications for the week could be:

MONDAY	— Write a thanksgiving prayer that can be prayed with the entire family on Thanksgiving Day.
TUESDAY	— Try to notice all the good things people do for you today and thank them.
WEDNESDAY	— Make a poster showing the things we are thankful for.
THURSDAY	— Collect food for the poor.
FRIDAY	— Write a letter to God, thanking him for himself, Jesus, and anything else you are thankful for.

H) **LITURGY OF THE EUCHARIST NOW TAKES PLACE:**

Procession

Students form an Offertory Procession and deposit food for the poor in containers.

Prayer Over the Gifts

"As we present our gifts, your gifts to you, may we realize that our brothers and sisters still go hungry. We ask this through Christ our Lord. Amen."

Prayer After Communion

"We have as our greatest gift, Father, your Son Jesus in Communion. Nourished by him, may we share this gift with others today."

SUGGESTED SONGS FOR A LITURGY ON THANKSGIVING:

"Sign of Total Giving"

"Whatsoever You Do"

"Take Our Bread"

"God Bless America"

"All That We Have"

"Look Beyond"

"America the Beautiful"

AFTER THE LITURGY

Banner — possible quotes:

1. I never think of you without thanking God.
2. What you are is God's gift to you. What you make of yourself is your gift to God.
3. Giving to others is a gift to self.
4. If you can't be thankful for what you receive, be thankful for what you escape.
5. For all that has been THANKS, for all that will be YES.

Application in School

The banner should be hung in its designated place, and the posters made and changed every day.

Biblical Readings

Some suggested readings for the week:

MONDAY — Luke 18:9-14

TUESDAY — Matthew 11:25-27

WEDNESDAY — John 11:41-42 — 2 Corinthians 14:16-19

THURSDAY — 1 Corinthians 14:16-19

FRIDAY — Romans 1:8-12

VARIATION

First Reading: Romans 1:8-12

NOTES:

_____
_____
_____
_____
_____
_____
_____
_____
_____
_____
_____

A Liturgy on Parents

THEME

Scripture says, "Honor your father and your mother, so that you may have a long life in the land that Yahweh your God has given to you." Today's liturgy will help us to reflect on the wonderful gift God gave us when he gave us our parents.

ORDER OF CELEBRATION

A) The celebrant processes down the main aisle of the church while the students sing an appropriate entrance hymn.

B) **PENITENTIAL RITE:**

    For not thanking you more for our fathers and mothers,

        LORD HAVE MERCY

    For not obeying our parents,

        CHRIST HAVE MERCY

    For the love our parents show to each other and us,

        LORD HAVE MERCY

C) **CELEBRANT READS AN APPROPRIATE PRAYER:**

    "Father, you made us in your own image. Send a blessing on all fathers and mothers because they show us love that is patterned on your love. They share love."

D) **FIRST READING:** Hebrews 12:5-13

E) **GOSPEL:** Luke 2:41-50

F) **HOMILY AND PRACTICAL ASPECTS:**

We should love our parents because they don't give us whatever we want, but what we really need. When parents give us what we need, they show that they really love us.

Some practical applications for the week may be:

MONDAY — During art period this week, make a gift for your parents.

TUESDAY — Obey your parents when they tell you to do something.

WEDNESDAY — Write a letter to your grandparents, or go and visit them.

THURSDAY — Ask your parents to share with you some of their memories of when they were waiting for you to be born and what you were like as a tiny newborn baby.

FRIDAY — Tonight before you go to bed, take time to tell your parents how much you really love them.

G) **LITURGY OF THE EUCHARIST NOW TAKES PLACE:**

Prayer Over the Gifts

"Father, you have offered us moments of joy and peace through our parents. Accept these gifts, that we may continue to be open to these moments."

Prayer After Communion

"Father, together we thank you for our mothers and fathers. May they give us an example by always doing your work."

SUGGESTED SONGS FOR LITURGY ON PARENTS:

"Rev. Mr. Black" (Kingston Trio)

"Some Day Soon" (Judy Collins)

"Trust and Obey" (John Fisher)

"Service"

"Yes, Lord"

"We Need Time"

"Day Is Done"

AFTER THE LITURGY

Banner — possible quotes:
1. Parents are the best present we ever get.
2. What a wonderful day.
3. We are shaped and fashioned by those we love.
4. God can't always be everywhere, and so he invented mothers.

Application in School
The banner should be hung in its designated place, and the posters made and changed every day.

Biblical Readings
Some suggested readings for the week:

MONDAY — 2 Timothy 3:2
TUESDAY — Ephesians 6:1
WEDNESDAY — Colossians 3:20
THURSDAY — Luke 2:41-50
FRIDAY — Hebrews 12:5-13

NOTES:

A Liturgy for Ash Wednesday and Lent

THEME

God sent Jonah to the people of Nineveh to tell them that they should do penance for their sins. Christ has sent his priest to remind us that we too should do penance. The coming of Lent will be a good time to think of those things in our lives that we are sorry for and to think of how to do better.

ORDER OF CELEBRATION

A) As the celebrant enters the church, an appropriate hymn is sung.

B) **PENITENTIAL RITE:**

You place your trust in us, and we do not really trust each other,

> LORD HAVE MERCY

You bid us spread peace, and our actions seek to divide,

> CHRIST HAVE MERCY

You have made us all brothers to one another, yet we pick and choose those we will love and those we will hate,

> LORD HAVE MERCY.

C) **CELEBRANT READS AN APPROPRIATE PRAYER:**

"Father, we stand before you; help us to love and not hate through these Lenten days."

D) **FIRST READING:** Jonah 3: 1-10

E) **GOSPEL READING:** Luke 13:1-5

F) **HOMILY AND PRACTICAL ASPECTS:**

If Lent is a time for a reevaluation of our lives as Christians, then we should not be looking at the negative aspects of Lent, such as *not* eating candy, *not* going to the movies, *not* watching television. Rather, we should see the positive aspects: I *will* listen to my parents, I *will* help with the dishes and housework, I *will* play with my brother and help him with his homework, I *will* be kinder to the people in school.

Some practical applications for this liturgy could be:

MONDAY — Think of one thing that keeps you from God and do something each day during Lent to improve on it.

TUESDAY — Pick one person that you may have hurt in some way and try to be especially kind to him during Lent.

WEDNESDAY — With the help of your teacher, study the story of Jonah and then work on a Jonah project for art class.

THURSDAY — Start a collection of symbols for Lent, Holy Week and Easter.

FRIDAY — Copy Psalm 22 and ask your parents to recite this with you during Lent.

G) **LITURGY OF THE EUCHARIST NOW TAKES PLACE:**

Prayer Over the Gifts

"Father, be pleased, accept this bread and wine as a sign that we are yours."

Prayer After Communion

"Father, you have given us a share in the Body of your Son in his life and death. Fill us once more with new strength and courage and make us one."

SUGGESTED SONGS FOR LITURGY FOR ASH WEDNESDAY AND LENT:

"Have Mercy, Lord" (FEL-II)

"May God Have Mercy" (Ray Repp)

"From the Depths" (FEL-II)
"Into Your Hands"
"Just a Closer Walk"
"Well, Well, Well"

AFTER THE LITURGY

Banner — possible quotes:
1. The day you no longer burn with love, many others will die of the cold.
2. The cares of today are often the joys of tomorrow.
3. Love grows best by giving it.

Application in School
1. The banner should be hung in its designated place, and the posters made and changed every day.
2. On Friday the celebrant could visit the school and examine the "Jonah Project."

Biblical Readings
Some suggested readings for the week:

MONDAY — Jonah 3:1-10
TUESDAY — Isaiah 58:1-9
WEDNESDAY — Joel 2:12-19
THURSDAY — Matthew 5:43-48 and 6:1-4
FRIDAY — Matthew 6:16-21

VARIATION

DISTRIBUTION OF ASHES FOR CHILDREN

The children should bring pencil and paper to church. On this paper they should write *one positive* thing they will do during Lent. They then process up the main aisle and deposit the paper in a brazier. The papers are then burnt and allowed to cool. The children later *take their own ashes* and sign themselves.

This is a "type" of covenant that a child makes between himself and God. It is known to no one. This may be much more meaningful to a child than to be given ashes.

NOTES:

_____
_____
_____
_____
_____
_____
_____
_____
_____
_____

A Liturgy on Ecology

THEME

This is a liturgy about the earth as our home. Today we look at men, animals, earth, water, and air . . . and our use and misuse of these gifts of God. How have we deprived people and destroyed the earth?

ORDER OF CELEBRATION

A) PENITENTIAL RITE:

> *(The Liturgy of the Word takes the form of several exorcisms. This implies an understanding of the existence and power of evil in the world. Such an understanding need not be bound to literal demons; in fact, the kind of ritual described here may be the best way of teaching that this is really only a way to talk about something which is very real but very hard to get a hold on. The exorcisms are such that they should speak to both children and adults, each group taking what it can from the words. There is no attempt to say that what's wrong with the environment is totally beyond man's control; rather, the exorcisms speak of overcoming evil by new acts and relationships.)*
>
> (From *Children's Liturgies,* edited by Virginia Sloyan and Gabe Huck. The Liturgical Conference, 1330 Massachusetts Ave., N.W., Washington, D.C. 20005. 1970.)

> Three children carry collages depicting the struggle between life and death. The children may wear costumes depicting the demons, but the costumes need not be elaborate. The collages should have

been prepared the week before by some of the children in school.

In the center aisle a trash barrel is provided, and each child as he enters the church should deposit his trash in the barrel. Children should be given time before the celebration to collect trash.

The celebrant enters after the children in procession and is accompanied by a cross-bearer and the three children carrying the collages.

The celebrant stops at the trash barrel for the rite.

PENITENTIAL RITE: Exorcisms of Pollutions

EXORCISM OF EARTH POLLUTION

"Depart, deadly spirit of pollution, from our earth. May we recognize you for what you are, an ever-growing threat to all life forms, to all that is created.

"You litter our landscape in various forms: paper, glass, metals, and plastics. With beer cans and car hulks, paper bags and non-returnables, with billboards and refuse dumps you cover our streets and highways. Beyond our vision you lurk in pesticides and poisons rained into our soil.

"But now, in an effort to restore our earth, we call on you to make way for a clean world. Begone in all the various forms of your deadly presence."

ALL: "OUT DEMONS, OUT!" *(Child places his collage near or against the trash barrel.)*

EXORCISM OF AIR POLLUTION

"Depart, deadly spirit of pollution, from our air and skies. May we recognize you for what you are, an ever-growing threat to all life forms, to all that is created.

"Your poisonous gases and harmful fumes are ever-present signs of you. Soot and ashes and deadly gases all give evidence of your pervading influence in our lives and of the many forms you take to disguise yourself from us.

"But now, in an effort to restore our air and sky, we call on you to make way for the bright rays of the sun and a freshness of air. Begone in all the various forms of your deadly presence."

ALL: "OUT DEMONS, OUT!" *(Child places his collage near or against the trash barrel.)*

EXORCISM OF WATER POLLUTION

"Depart, deadly spirit of pollution, from our waters. May we recognize you for what you are, an ever-growing threat to all life forms, to all that is created.

"You take the forms of phosphates and various industrial wastes. You come from our kitchen sinks and from the giant factories and municipal sewage plants. The heat of nuclear reactors on our waters makes them sources of death for the flowers and fish of the sea. You do all this in the name of progress.

"But now, in an effort to restore our rivers and seas and oceans, we call on you to make way for the clean, refreshing waters. Begone in all the forms of your presence."

ALL: "OUT DEMONS, OUT!" *(Child places his collage near or against the trash barrel.)*

(An appropriate hymn is now sung, such as "This Land Is Your Land" or "America the Beautiful.")

C) **CELEBRANT READS AN APPROPRIATE PRAYER:**

"Father, our streams, air, and earth are polluted by big industries. We ourselves throw gum wrappers and cold drink cans along the highway. Please help us to remember that this land is our land. We ask this through Christ Our Lord. Amen."

D) **FIRST READING:**

CANTICLE TO ALL CREATION

by St. Francis

Be praised, my Lord, with all your created things.
Be praised for brother sun, who brings the day and gives us light. He is fair and radiant with a shining face and he draws his meaning from on high.

Be praised, my Lord, for sister moon and the stars. In the heavens you have made them clear and precious and lovely.

Be praised, my Lord, for our brother wind, and for the air and clouds and calm days and every kind of weather by which you give your creatures nourishment.

Be praised, my Lord, for our sister water, which is very helpful and humble, precious and pure.

Be praised, my Lord, for our brother fire, by which you light up the darkness: he is fair and gay and mighty and strong.

Be praised, my Lord, for our mother earth, for she sustains and keeps us, and brings forth all kinds of fruits together with the grasses and bright flowers.

Be praised, my Lord, for our sister, bodily death, from which no living man can flee.

Be praised, my Lord, for all creatures. We give you thanks.

D) **GOSPEL READING:** Matthew 6:25-29

E) **HOMILY AND PRACTICAL APPLICATIONS:**
God has made all the beautiful things — water, land, mountains, etc. The most beautiful thing he made is man. But look what man has done — he has polluted creation. If this earth is made for us to enjoy, what are we doing when we throw gum wrappers, cold drink cans, bottles and rocks?

Some practical applications for the liturgy may be:

MONDAY — With the help of your teacher, clean certain areas around school or in town that are eyesores.

TUESDAY — Write a letter to the mayor about a major pollution problem in town and ask him to appoint a committee to do something about this problem. A box will be placed in your classroom to collect the letters and someone appointed to mail them.

WEDNESDAY — Draw a picture of the most beautiful or the ugliest thing in town; an award will be given for the best picture. Perhaps the picture could be included in the letter going to the mayor's office. All pictures should be displayed on two bulletin boards.

THURSDAY — Thoroughly clean your bedroom today. Get rid of all those old papers.

FRIDAY — Help the teacher clean the schoolroom, and you clean your own desk.

F) **LITURGY OF THE EUCHARIST NOW TAKES PLACE:**

Prayer Over the Gifts

"Father, accept our gifts of bread and wine. Make us preserve the gifts you have given us on earth. This we ask through Christ Our Lord. Amen."

Prayer After Communion

"Father, we give you thanks for Jesus in Communion. May we be thankful also for the richness, productiveness and beauty of our land."

SUGGESTED SONGS FOR THE LITURGY ON ECOLOGY:

"New Creation"

"I Lift Up My Eyes"

"How Long, O Lord?"

"Priestly People"

"Sing Out, O Sion"

"Love Is Surrender" (Carpenters)

"The Spirit Is a-Movin' "

AFTER THE LITURGY

Banner — possible quotes:

1. Give thanks to him, bless his name.
2. I just want to be there — in love and in justice, and in truth and in commitment to others, so that we can make of this old world a new world.
3. Earth, air, and seas, bless the Lord.
4. Did you know that the word "American" ends in I Can?

Application in School

1. The banner should be hung in its designated place, and the posters made and changed every day.
2. On Tuesday someone should be appointed to mail the letters to the mayor.
3. On Friday the celebrant should visit the rooms to see the pictures that the students have started to draw. If students do not have enough time to finish this project, they should complete it next Friday.

Biblical Readings

Some suggested readings for the week:

    MONDAY   — Genesis 1:1-31 and 2:1-4

TUESDAY	— Psalm 65
WEDNESDAY	— Genesis 8:15-22
THURSDAY	— Luke 12:22-27
FRIDAY	— Psalm 66 and 67

Alternate Reading: Genesis 1:1-31

NOTES:

_____

_____

_____

_____

_____

_____

_____

_____

_____

_____

A Liturgy on Celebrating

THEME

Today we celebrate a liturgy that wishes to remind us of the necessity of being joyful and of marking events in our lives with joy and ceremony. Let us make this day a joyful celebration.

ORDER OF CELEBRATION

A) The celebrant does not process up the aisle, but is seated for a reading:

    THE ABILITY TO LAUGH

"It has long been my belief that one of the things which have enabled man to survive is the ability to laugh. No matter how difficult the situation may be, man somehow has always been able to find humor in his situation.
If I were given the opportunity to present a gift to the next generation, it would be the ability for each individual to learn to laugh at himself.
I have not always had this ability, but have envied those who do, and I think it is one of God's greatest blessings."

    Excerpted from "A Conversation with Charles Schulz" by Mary Harrington Hall, *Psychology Today* magazine, January 1968. Copyright © Communications/Research/Machines, Inc.

B) **PENITENTIAL RITE:**

    For not helping people to be full of joy,

        LORD HAVE MERCY

For not making every moment of our life a celebration,
> CHRIST HAVE MERCY

For not recognizing the need to be joyful,
> LORD HAVE MERCY

C) **CELEBRANT READS AN APPROPRIATE PRAYER:**

"Father, today we come to celebrate your Son's death/rising which brings us joy. May we realize that he brings joy which surpasses any joys that are known."

D) **FIRST READING:** Psalm 150

E) **GOSPEL READING:** Luke 10:17-20

F) **HOMILY AND PRACTICAL ASPECTS:**

Maybe birthday celebrations and any other occasions worthy of celebration could be discussed. It is hoped that this homily would lead the children to see the importance of liturgical celebrations that involve events in the life of Christ.

Some practical aspects for the week could be:

MONDAY	— Search out the small, beautiful things in life usually overlooked.
TUESDAY	— Make joyful instruments in art class today.
WEDNESDAY	— Make a list of "joyful" celebrations that you remembered and enjoyed.
THURSDAY	— Pray that God will always help you to be a joyful person.
FRIDAY	— If you see anyone who is not joyful today, see if there is anything you can do to make him more joyful.

G) **LITURGY OF THE EUCHARIST NOW TAKES PLACE:**

Prayer Over the Gifts

"Father, take this bread and wine and the prayers that we voice as a sign that we are yours, children full of joy."

Prayer After Communion

"Father, having broken bread together, let us recall that our life with others and your Son is a life of joy."

SUGGESTED SONGS FOR LITURGY ON CELEBRATING:
"Gonna Sing My Lord"
"King of Glory"
"Joy, Joy, Joy"
"I Am the Resurrection"
"The Spirit Is a-Movin' "
"I Lift Up My Eyes"

AFTER THE LITURGY

Banner — possible quote:

Of all things you wear, your expression is the most important.

Application in School

1. The banner should be hung in its designated place and the posters made and changed every day.
2. The celebrant should visit the school and look at the instruments the children made in art class.

Biblical Readings

Some suggested readings for the week:

MONDAY — Psalm 96
TUESDAY — Psalm 97
WEDNESDAY — Psalm 148
THURSDAY — Psalm 138
FRIDAY — Psalm 135

NOTES:

_____
_____
_____
_____
_____

A Liturgy on Hope

THEME

"I believe in the resurrection of the dead, and the life of the world to come." We trust that we will obtain from God all that he has promised, especially our eternal happiness. Today we will spend some time thinking about hope.

ORDER OF CELEBRATION

A) The celebrant processes down the aisle while the students sing an appropriate song.

B) **PENITENTIAL RITE:**

   That you are the sign of our hope,

       LORD HAVE MERCY

   That hope is never lost in our life,

       CHRIST HAVE MERCY

   That the poor and lonely see hope in you,

       LORD HAVE MERCY

C) **CELEBRANT READS AN APPROPRIATE PRAYER:**

   "Father, our hope is that we accept what we cannot understand or understand what we find hard to accept."

D) **FIRST READING:**

A FAR DEEPER HOPE

There are two kinds of hope. First, the hope of success, which gives men daring, and helps them win against odds. That isn't the best sort of hope. It's dangerous, like drug-taking. You must keep on increasing the dose, and blindfolding your reason. Men who do it are buoyant, self-confident, but some of their integrity is lost.

The best kind of hope is not about success in this or that undertaking. It's far deeper; hence when things go against you, it isn't destroyed. It is hope about the nature and future of man and the universe.

(Clarence Day, from *Listen to Love* by Louis M. Savary, S.J. Published by The Regina Press, Hicksville, N.Y. 11801.)

E) **GOSPEL READING:** Matthew 12:15-21

F) **HOMILY AND PRACTICAL ASPECTS:**
There are many things in life we cannot understand. Children especially have trouble understanding why they don't always succeed in their undertakings, why they don't "win the ball game." Hope in God gives us the means whereby we can accept what we cannot understand.

Some practical applications for the week could be:

MONDAY	— Draw a picture of the symbol of hope and give the story of the symbol.
TUESDAY	— Help clean up the yard at home.
WEDNESDAY	— Pray today for the virtue of hope.
THURSDAY	— Discuss with your teacher what it means to "accept what we cannot understand."
FRIDAY	— Visit some lonely person today.

G) **LITURGY OF THE EUCHARIST NOW TAKES PLACE:**

Prayer Over the Gifts

"Father, we offer you bread and wine with the hope that we can see that Jesus is with us."

Prayer After Communion

"Father, sharing in the meal gives us hope that we can give ourselves to you and to others."

SUGGESTED SONGS FOR LITURGY ON HOPE
"All My Trials"
"And I Will Follow"
"How Long, O Lord?"
"In You O Lord, I Place My Trust"
"Put Your Hand in the Hand"
"Day Is Done"

AFTER THE LITURGY

Banner — possible quote:

Some men see things as they are and say "Why?" I dream of things that never were and say "Why Not?"

Application in School

The banner should be hung in its designated place, and the posters changed every day.

Biblical Readings

Some suggested readings for the week:

MONDAY — Philippians 1:9-11
TUESDAY — Philippians 3:8-11
WEDNESDAY — Philippians 4:4-9
THURSDAY — Matthew 25:31-46
FRIDAY — John 14:1-3

VARIATION

FIRST READING: Isaiah 43:1,2

NOTES:

_____

_____

_____

_____

A Liturgy on Sharing

THEME

Sharing means experiencing and enjoying something with other people. It also means taking part in some activity with others. Let's think today about what it means to share, and ask ourselves whether we are really willing to share with others.

ORDER OF CELEBRATION

A) The celebrant processes down the aisle while the students sing an appropriate song.

B) **PENITENTIAL RITE:**

> For lack of willingness to give,
>
> > LORD HAVE MERCY
>
> For taking instead of giving,
>
> > CHRIST HAVE MERCY
>
> For a willingness to give help to others,
>
> > LORD HAVE MERCY

C) **CELEBRANT READS AN APPROPRIATE PRAYER:**

> "Father, as we gather here this morning, may we learn to share ourselves with others."

D) **FIRST READING:**

"But light is for communication. Let your light so shine before men that they may see your good works and glorify your Father who is in heaven. In terms of ordinary living this means that if you are really looking for truth, your own discoveries about it will affect your behavior, will make you 'clearer' to other people so that they will see the point of being committed to something more than getting through life from day to day without actual harm or misery, and will be encouraged in their own efforts. Light, in fact, is essentially a communal thing; it is of its nature to be shared."

(Rosemary Haughton, from *Listen to Love* by Louis M. Savary, S.J. The Regina Press, Hicksville, N.Y. 11801. 1970.)

E) **GOSPEL READING:** Matthew 15:32-39

F) **HOMILY AND PRACTICAL ASPECTS:**

Sharing is a gift of self. Sharing is not only a giving of *something* you like to another, but a giving of self, of time. The child begins to mature when he realizes that besides himself there exist others. At this moment he gives of himself willingly—he shares.

Some practical applications for the week could be:

MONDAY — Bring something to school tomorrow to share with someone you have never shared with before.

TUESDAY — Share some of the housework with your parents tonight.

WEDNESDAY — Share your knowledge today. Help someone with his homework or classwork.

THURSDAY — Say a special prayer today that God would help you to be very generous in sharing with other people.

FRIDAY — Do something nice for the priests today.

G) **LITURGY OF THE EUCHARIST NOW TAKES PLACE:**

Prayer Over the Gifts

"Father, we give you our gifts; may we give ourselves totally to you and others."

Prayer After Communion

"Father, you have given us your Son, Jesus. May he, whom you have given to us, be shared with others."

SUGGESTED SONGS FOR LITURGY ON SHARING

"Service"

"Less of Me"

"Take Our Bread"

"All That We Have"

"Canticle of the Gift"

AFTER THE LITURGY

Banner — possible quotes:

1. Love is not love until you give it away.
2. The best gift is a part of self.
3. Coming together is a beginning; keeping together is progress; working together is success.

Application in School

The banner should be hung in its designated place and the posters changed every day.

Biblical Readings

Some suggested readings for the week:

    MONDAY — Exodus 29:26-28

    TUESDAY — Exodus 18:13-23

    WEDNESDAY — Matthew 5:1-10

    THURSDAY — Luke 6:27-35

    FRIDAY — Matthew 15:32-39

VARIATION

Exodus 18:13-23

NOTES:

A Liturgy on Speaking

THEME

When we speak we express our feelings and our ideas to others. Sometimes we can do so much good by speaking the right word at the right time, and sometimes we hurt others so deeply when we refuse to speak to them. Today at this Eucharistic celebration, we want to consider "speaking."

ORDER OF CELEBRATION

A) The celebrant is seated and everyone listens to a recording with the words of the song "Sounds of Silence."

B) **PENITENTIAL RITE:**

> For being hesitant in speaking your words,
>
> > LORD HAVE MERCY
>
> For not speaking to a person who irritates us,
>
> > CHRIST HAVE MERCY
>
> For not realizing that words help to unite people,
>
> > LORD HAVE MERCY

C) **CELEBRANT READS AN APPROPRIATE PRAYER:**

> "Father, you speak to us through words of the bible. May we always listen to your words."

D) **FIRST READING:** 1 Corinthians 13:1-3

E) **GOSPEL READING:** John 12:44-50

F) **HOMILY AND PRACTICAL ASPECTS:**
Actions can express or communicate a thought as well as or better than words. But speaking is the communication or sharing of self with another. It is an exchange of persons through dialogue.

Some practical applications for the week could be:

MONDAY	— Listen today in class when someone is speaking.
TUESDAY	— Write a letter to God, telling how much you love him.
WEDNESDAY	— Don't talk out of turn today.
THURSDAY	— During recess today speak to people that you don't usually talk to on the school ground.
FRIDAY	— Say something nice to your teacher and your parents.

G) **LITURGY OF THE EUCHARIST NOW TAKES PLACE:**

Prayer Over the Gifts

"Father, may these gifts we offer you be signs of us speaking to you."

Prayer After Communion

"Father, by sharing in the Eucharist, we have responded to your spoken word. May we go forth to speak and share your words with others."

SUGGESTED SONGS FOR LITURGY ON SPEAKING

"We Are One in the Spirit"

"Spirit Is a-Movin' "

"Shout Out Your Joy"

"Sing Out His Goodness"

"Tell the World"

"Get Together"

"Go Tell It on the Mountain"

"Sounds of Silence" (recording)

AFTER THE LITURGY

Banner — possible quotes:

1. What you are speaks so loud, I cannot hear what you are saying.
2. Loving is listening.

Application in School

The banner should be hung in its designated place, and the posters changed every day.

Biblical Readings

Some suggested readings for the week:

MONDAY — Matthew 23:3
TUESDAY — Matthew 15:11
WEDNESDAY — Matthew 10:19,20
THURSDAY — Luke 12:11
FRIDAY — Acts 2:1-13

NOTES:

A Liturgy on the Ascension

THEME

This is the day we celebrate the transfer of the risen body of Christ from this earth.

ORDER OF CELEBRATION

A) The celebrant enters and the students greet him with a song.

B) **PENITENTIAL RITE:**

> For not showing belief in you, Lord, by speech and action,
>> LORD HAVE MERCY

> For not doing your work of rebuilding your cities,
>> CHRIST HAVE MERCY

> For not having all men as our brothers,
>> LORD HAVE MERCY

C) **CELEBRANT READS AN APPROPRIATE PRAYER:**

> "Father, you have taken your Son to sit at your right hand until he comes again. We ask for your blessing while our hands are set to the task of building a city of peace and a land where men can live as brothers."

D) **FIRST READING:** Acts 1:6-11

E) **GOSPEL READING:** Luke 24:50-53

F) **HOMILY AND POSSIBLE ASPECTS:**
If Jesus is no longer here in his visible humanity, then someone has to carry on his work, to spread peace and joy. This is now our work, in the family, in the school, in the community. Have we really taken our job seriously? Have we been spreading peace and joy?

Some practical applications for the week could be:

MONDAY	— Spread joy at home by not fighting with your brothers and sisters today.
TUESDAY	— Walk quietly on the stairs and in the halls today.
WEDNESDAY	— Pray that we live true peaceful lives full of joy.
THURSDAY	— During art period today, draw the picture of the Ascension.
FRIDAY	— Write a song in honor of the Ascension.

G) **LITURGY OF THE EUCHARIST NOW TAKES PLACE:**

Prayer Over the Gifts

"Father, look upon these gifts of bread and wine, which we offer in your sight as we continue to spread your message."

Prayer After Communion

"Father, we don't know when your Son will come again. Let us not stand by idle, for there is much for us to do."

SUGGESTED SONGS FOR LITURGY ON THE ASCENSION:

"Peace, My Friends"

"Shalom"

"Clap Your Hands"

"New Creation"

AFTER THE LITURGY

Banner — possible quotes:

1. Shalom.
2. I am going to get a place ready for you.

Application in School

The banner should be hung in its designated place, and the posters changed every day.

Biblical Readings

Some suggested readings for the week:

> MONDAY — Acts 1:1-11
> TUESDAY — Matthew 24:30-31
> WEDNESDAY — Revelation 14:14-16
> THURSDAY — Acts 2:29-36
> FRIDAY — John 3:12-15

NOTES:

A Liturgy on Freedom

THEME

To be happy, a person needs to be free not to do just anything, but free to be truly human. Many times people are not free because we will not let them be. Today, let us think about our freedom.

ORDER OF CELEBRATION

A) The celebrant processes up the main aisle while the students sing an appropriate entrance hymn.

B) **PENITENTIAL RITE:**

    We will not be free until all people are free,

        LORD HAVE MERCY

For man's thoughtless use of creation, and the fear of destruction from nuclear weapons,

        CHRIST HAVE MERCY

For a world that doesn't allow women equal rights,

        LORD HAVE MERCY

C) **AN APPROPRIATE PRAYER IS READ:**

"Father, there is no better way of showing our thanks than by sharing your gift of freedom with our fellowmen. Help us to live out this belief."

D) **FIRST READING:**

READ THEM OVER

Read them over, the great documents of the past;
The Bill of Rights, the Gettysburg Address,
The Declaration of Independence — these
should steel the heart through any time of stress.

The truth lies in them, faith and hope are there,
Too long we have gone groping on our way,
We need the clarion call of the clear words,
We need a valiant leader for our day.

And we would live for freedom or would die
That slavery be abolished from the earth.
We have a subtle slavery today,
and fail to recognize its slow sure birth.

America, our land, we would be free.
Shake off the burdens of the recent years.
May all the lands be unshackled of their bonds,
and freed at last from dark and torturing fears.

(From *Let the Sun Shine In* by Grace Noll Crowell. Copyright © 1970 by Fleming H. Revell Company. Used by permission.)

E) **GOSPEL READING:** John 8:31-38

F) **HOMILY AND PRACTICAL ASPECTS:**

By freedom, we do not mean license. Freedom is a mutual thing; it is not thrusting your ideas, or your way of doing things, or your way of thinking on another person or another person's ideas. Freedom is letting others develop themselves as they are — freely. Our freedom can be taken away from us when we misuse it by destroying the rights of others.

Some practical applications may be:

MONDAY — Clean up your room without anyone asking you to.

TUESDAY — Start working on a scrapbook that contains positive ideas of freedom.

WEDNESDAY — Pray that we realize we will be free only when all people are free and that only we can free others. God will not force us.

THURSDAY — Discuss in class today what it means to "be free and obey the school rules."

FRIDAY — Do something for someone that will help free him to be more human.

G) LITURGY OF THE EUCHARIST NOW TAKES PLACE:

Prayer Over the Gifts

"Father, the gifts we offer at this Mass, bread and wine, although hardly impressive in themselves, are acceptable to you because they are offered by men who are free."

Prayer After Communion

"Father, may we prove worthy of your invitation of love — men responsible enough to use our freedom for others and to the glory of your name."

SUGGESTED SONGS FOR LITURGY ON FREEDOM:

"If I Had a Hammer"

"Come Away"

"Have You Ever Been"

"We Shall Overcome"

"Declaration of Independence" (Fifth Dimension)

AFTER THE LITURGY

Banner — possible quotes:

1. Wisdom is to learn to live with ourselves and others.
2. God gives his people strength.
3. What in the world are you doing for heaven's sake?
4. Freedom Now.

Application in School

1. The banner should be hung in its designated place, and the posters made and changed every day.
2. On Friday, the celebrant could go to the classrooms, visit the children and look at their scrapbooks.

Biblical Readings

Some suggested readings for the week:

MONDAY — Galatians 3:13-14
TUESDAY — Romans 8:1-17
WEDNESDAY — Luke 4:18-22
THURSDAY — John 8:31-38
FRIDAY — Exodus 6:6

VARIATION

First reading: Romans 8:1-11

NOTES:

_____
_____
_____
_____
_____
_____
_____
_____
_____
_____

A Liturgy on Listening

THEME

(To be announced by a student.)

Today's liturgy focuses on listening. To listen means to make a conscious effort to hear. It also means a willingness to take advice. Today we will reflect on the times in our lives when God spoke to us and we listened, or maybe we refused to listen.

ORDER OF CELEBRATION

A) As the celebrant enters the church, an entrance hymn is sung.

B) **PENITENTIAL RITE:**

    We have failed to listen attentively to our Father's voice,

        LORD HAVE MERCY

    For not listening to our parents, teachers and friends,

        CHRIST HAVE MERCY

    For the times that our ears listened, but our minds refused to accept the good advice God and our friends were offering,

        LORD HAVE MERCY

C) **CELEBRANT READS AN APPROPRIATE PRAYER:**

"Father, as we gather here today, may we listen carefully to your words in the bible, in order that we might hear the cry of the needy — our brothers."

D) **CELEBRANT ANNOUNCES:**

("We will now listen to a record. The words of this record tell us something about people who hear but don't listen.") The record player may be set up in the sanctuary, or anyplace near a microphone in order that the recording may be heard by everyone in the church. Record: *The Sounds of Silence,* by P. Simon, of Simon and Garfunkel, copyright Charing Cross Music Inc.

E) **FIRST READING:** Romans 10:14-16

F) **GOSPEL:** John 8:42-47

G) **HOMILY AND PRACTICAL ASPECTS:**

A distinction between hearing and listening: Listening focuses one's *whole* attention on the speaker. We listen to a person because we respect and care for the person. Too often hearing implies only an auditory reflex. We want to listen, not only hear.

There should be a dialogue homily with the children. There are some good points mentioned in the song, "Sounds of Silence," especially the lines "people hearing without listening," and "hear my words that I might teach you" and "the words of the prophets are written on the subway walls, and whisper in the sounds of silence" — no one to hear.

Some practical applications for the week may be:

MONDAY — Listen how God speaks to you. Maybe your teacher could help you with this project.

TUESDAY — Listen, and do what your parents tell you this week without question.

WEDNESDAY — Make a special effort to listen in school this week.

THURSDAY — Listen to the sounds of God's creation and make a list of them. When it is your turn for the class Mass, bring up the list at the offertory procession.

FRIDAY — Listen when a friend speaks to you today and try to remember what he said.

H) LITURGY OF THE EUCHARIST NOW TAKES PLACE:

Prayer Over the Gifts

"Father, our gifts are on your table. May we listen to your word that makes our life meaningful."

Prayer After Communion

"By receiving your Son's Body and Blood, may we listen more to others and to your word."

SUGGESTED SONGS FOR LITURGY ON LISTENING:

"Sing Praise to the Lord"

"Look Beyond"

"Yes, Lord"

"Try a Little Kindness"

"Blowing in the Wind"

"Sounds of Silence"

AFTER THE LITURGY

Banner — possible quotes:

1. I can't hear you because of what I expect you to say.
2. Your actions speak so loud, I can't hear what you are saying.
3. Please listen to me.
4. Hear me; I'm calling.

Application in School

1. The banner should be hung in its designated place, and the posters changed every day.
2. Teachers will try to prepare children for the offertory procession by seeing to it that the class prepares its list of sounds.

Biblical Readings

Some suggested readings for the week:

MONDAY — John 9:24-38

TUESDAY — Matthew 10:26-33

WEDNESDAY — Mark 8:14-21

THURSDAY — Revelation 18:21-24

FRIDAY — Romans 10:14-18 and John 8:43-47

NOTES:

_____
_____
_____
_____
_____
_____
_____
_____
_____
_____

A Liturgy on Time

THEME

John Donne once wrote:
God made sun and moon to distinguish seasons,
and day and night,
and we cannot have the fruits of the earth
but in their seasons;
but God hath made no decree to distinguish the seasons
of his mercies;
in paradise the fruits were ripe the first minute,
and in heaven it is always autumn,
his mercies are ever at their maturity.
God never says you should have come yesterday;
but today he will hear you.
He brought light out of darkness,
not out of lesser light;
he can bring your summer out of winter,
though you have no spring.
All occasions invite his mercies,
and all times are his seasons.

ORDER OF CELEBRATION

A) The celebrant enters the church in perfect silence. When he has reached the presidential chair, the guitars or whatever instruments are used in the celebration play softly "Turn, Turn, Turn," or "The Love Theme From Romeo and Juliet." While this is being played, a reader reads from Ecclesiastes 3:1-8.

B) **PENITENTIAL RITE:**

    For wasting time by just sitting around,

        LORD HAVE MERCY

    For not recognizing that there isn't much time in our lives,

        CHRIST HAVE MERCY

    For the time we spent just talking and not acting,

        LORD HAVE MERCY

C) **CELEBRANT READS AN APPROPRIATE PRAYER:**

    "Father, grant that we, like your Son Jesus, may redeem the time that you have given us."

D) **FIRST READING:**

    When do you start caring? And what do you start caring about?
    What is time? How is yesterday different from tomorrow?
    How far back can you remember? Before kindergarten? What do you remember?
    What did you care about most when you were in the first and second grades?
    How did your interests change between then and now?
    How have you changed between then and now?
    Do you really believe that you'll be settled by the time you're 21? Why?
    "This may be the day to start caring"
    about wrinkles or pimples on your skin?
    about dry hair or a bad figure?
    about making friends?
    about facing the questions?
    about other people?
    Is there anything worth caring for now?
    Will it be easier to care tomorrow?
    Is this "instant success" or success for the instant?
    And is success for the instant really success at all?
    What kind of success am I really looking for in my life?
    What kind of success can make me really happy — not just for now, but for a while?

        (From *Discovery in Advertising*, Richard J. Payne and Robert Heyer, S.J., Paulist Press, New York, 1969.)

E) **GOSPEL READING:** John 7:1-7

F) **HOMILY AND PRACTICAL ASPECTS:**
There should be a dialogue homily with the students. Two values to be impressed upon the students: 1) they must realize that time is precious and should not be wasted; we should all "get involved." 2) When it comes to people, there must always be time spent in assisting or helping, whenever they need us.

Some practical applications for the week could be:

MONDAY — Spend time this week making sad people happy.

TUESDAY — Stop talking about your work today and do it; especially any work that you have deliberately neglected.

WEDNESDAY — Pray today that everybody may realize that time on earth is to be spent for others.

THURSDAY — Make a large collage from the scripture reading, Ecclesiastes 3:1-8.

FRIDAY — Spend some of your time today visiting some old people who find "time" long and lonely.

G) **LITURGY OF THE EUCHARIST NOW TAKES PLACE:**

Prayer Over the Gifts

"Father, as we present this bread and wine to you, may we take time to reflect on your presence with us."

Prayer After Communion

"Father, having broken bread together, may we leave this place and use our time in bringing you to all men."

SUGGESTED SONGS FOR A LITURGY ON TIME:

"We Need Time"

"Man of Mind"

"Service"

"Born to Live and Die"

"Put Your Hand in the Hand"

"How Long, O Lord?"

"Pause a While"

"Turn, Turn, Turn"

AFTER THE LITURGY

Banner — possible quotes:
1. Lord, I have time.
2. A Time. . .
3. A time to love.

Application in School
The banner should be hung in its designated place, and the posters changed every day.

Biblical Readings
Some suggested readings for the week:

MONDAY — Matthew 27:24-33
TUESDAY — Matthew 13:28-39
WEDNESDAY — Matthew 16:1-4 and 12:38-39
THURSDAY — 1 Corinthians 11:23, 24 and 2 Corinthians 6:1-10
FRIDAY — John 16:16-22

VARIATION
First Reading: 2 Corinthians 6:1-11

NOTES:

A Liturgy on Epiphany

THEME

This is the day we celebrate Jesus' revealing himself to the Gentile nations in the persons of the Wise Men.

ORDER OF CELEBRATION

A) The celebrant enters the church accompanied by three children dressed as Wise Men. One child carries the bread, another the wine, and the third child carries a large candle, not lighted. The students may sing "We Three Kings." When the singing is over, the last child places the candle in the middle of the altar and lights it. (No other candle is used for the celebration.) Immediately after, there is a reading:

A GREAT LIGHT

The people who walked in darkness
have seen a great light;
those who dwelt in a land of deep darkness,
on them has light shined.
For to us a child is born,
to us a son is given;
and the government will be upon his shoulder,
and his name will be called
"Wonderful, Counselor, Mighty God,
Everlasting Father, Prince of Peace."
Of the increase of his government
and of peace
there will be no end,

upon the throne of David,
and over his kingdom, to establish it,
and to uphold it with justice
and with righteousness
from this time forth and for evermore.

(Isaiah 9:2-7)

B) **PENITENTIAL RITE:**

That we may be a light to your presence,
> LORD HAVE MERCY

That we remember you are light of the world,
> CHRIST HAVE MERCY

That we have doubted you and others,
> LORD HAVE MERCY

C) **CELEBRANT READS AN APPROPRIATE PRAYER:**

"Father, the three Wise Men were sent so that all men might see that your Son is the light of the world. Open our eyes that we may recognize you in all the signs which you send us."

D) **FIRST READING:** Isaiah 60:1-6

E) **GOSPEL READING:** Matthew 2:1-12

F) **HOMILY AND PRACTICAL ASPECTS:**

The presence of Jesus is not only reserved in the tabernacle — in the church building — but Jesus is present in each man. Therefore we must deliver his message of *love* to all men. Children should see the symbolism of the lighted candle as their love and good works helping other people, as any light helps people who are in the dark.

Some practical applications may be:

MONDAY — Let us show today and all this week that our "light" to be given to others is our kindness to one another.

TUESDAY — Pray today that we may be more trusting of other people, especially our teachers and classmates.

WEDNESDAY — Decorate a pretty box in art class for your mother and give it to her as a gift.

THURSDAY — Ask mother if she would give you a "King Cake Party."

FRIDAY — "Let your light shine" today in the cafeteria — be good.

G) LITURGY OF THE EUCHARIST NOW TAKES PLACE:

(The three children dressed in the costumes of the kings will bring up the gifts this day.)

Prayer Over the Gifts

"Father, from east and west, north and south, we offer your gifts and sing your praise. We ask you to bless us with the gifts of your Son that we may be signs to all men that you are always with us."

Prayer After Communion

"Father, may we who have broken bread together, be signs of your peace in our world and may we who have received your gift of love proclaim that love to all men."

SUGGESTED SONG FOR LITURGY FOR EPIPHANY:

"We Three Kings"

AFTER THE LITURGY

Banner — possible quote:

Our love for God is tested by the question of whether we seek him, or his gifts.

Application in School

The banner should be hung in its designated place, and the posters changed every day.

Biblical Readings

(Genesis 2:7)

Some suggested readings for the week:

MONDAY — 1 Corinthians 1:7
TUESDAY — 1 Corinthians 12:7
WEDNESDAY — 2 Corinthians 4:2

THURSDAY — John 2:11
FRIDAY — John 17:6

NOTES:

_____
_____
_____
_____
_____
_____
_____
_____
_____
_____

A Liturgy for Halloween and Saints' Days

THEME

Often we spend time thinking of heroes. Today we will spend some time thinking about heroes and saints of the Church. We wish to congratulate all these saints and heroes and remind ourselves that the whole world awaits their return.

ORDER OF CELEBRATION

A) The celebrant processes down the main aisle. With him are 15 small children dressed in costumes depicting Saints Peter, Paul, Philip the Apostle, Andrew the Apostle, John the Apostle, Luke, Matthew, James, Bartholomew, Mark, Thomas, Jude and Simon, James, and Matthias.

B) **PENITENTIAL RITE:**

You have called us your children,
   LORD HAVE MERCY

You have shown us how to lead a Christian life,
   CHRIST HAVE MERCY

You have patiently loved us in spite of our faults,
   LORD HAVE MERCY

C) CELEBRANT READS AN APPROPRIATE PRAYER:

"Father, we rejoice today in the countless number of people who have gone ahead of us and enjoy the vision of you. Help us to imitate their lives of courage and dedication to Jesus' good news."

D) FIRST READING:

(The music from "Abraham, Martin, and John" or "Lonesome Valley" could be played in the background softly.)

O CAPTAIN! MY CAPTAIN!

O Captain! My Captain! Our fearful trip is done,
The ship has weather'd every rack, the prize we sought is won,
The port is near, the bells I hear, the people all exulting,
While follow eyes the steady keel, the vessel grim and daring;

> But O heart! heart! heart!
> O the bleeding drops of red,
> Where on the deck my Captain lies,
> fallen cold and dead.

O Captain! My Captain! rise up and hear the bells;
Rise up — for you the flag is flung — for you the bugle trills,
For you bouquets and ribboned wreaths — for you the shores a-crowding
For you they call, the swaying mass, their eager faces turning;

> Hear Captain! dear father!
> The arm beneath your head!
> It is some dream that on the deck,
> You've fallen cold and dead.

My captain does not answer, his lips are pale and still,
My father does not feel my arm, he has no pulse nor will,
The ship is anchored safe and sound, its voyage closed and done,
From fearful trip the victor ship comes in with object won;

> Exult O shores, and ring O bells!
> But I with mournful tread,
> Walk the deck my Captain lies,
> Fallen cold and dead.

(Walt Whitman)

RESPONSORIAL PSALM:

(The children seated on the left-hand side of the church recite the left-hand verse and alternate with the children on the right-hand side. Left-hand side begins.)

    Prince of Apostles   Rock of the faith
    Red flow the banners ho! keeper of the keys
    Sing of the glory: and evermore shall be so.

(Child dressed as Peter gets up and stands in the aisle.)

    Paul of the Gentiles   Father to the pagan and Jew:
    Red flow the banners ho! Giver of the life of God.
    Sing of the glory:

(Child dressed as Paul gets up and stands in the aisle.)

    Philip the Apostle   Come see the Savior.
    Red flow the banners ho!
    Sing of the glory:

(Child dressed as Philip gets up and stands in the aisle.)

    Andrew the Apostle   Bring to the Lord thy brother.
    Red flow the banners ho!
    Sing of the glory:

    John the Apostle   Eagle in flight to the heights of God.
    Red flow the banners ho!
    Sing of the glory:

    Luke beloved doctor   Scribe at the feet of Mary.
    Red flow the banners ho!
    Sing of the glory:

    Matthew the Apostle   Torch of the faith in the land of the sun.
    Red flow the banners ho!
    Sing of the glory:

    James of Jerusalem   Chief in the land of Jesus.
    Red flow the banners ho!
    Sing of the glory:

    Next is Bartholomew   Slayed by the knife that gave him life.
    Red flow the banners ho!
    Sing of the glory:

    Mark the holy writer   Pen for the words of Peter.
    Red flow the banners ho!
    Sing of the glory:

Thomas the doubtful
Red flow the banners ho!
Sing of the glory:

Blessed are they who shall believe.

James the Apostle
Red flow the banners ho!
Sing of the glory:

Two were the sons of thunder.

Now Jude and Simon
Red flow the banners ho!
Sing of the glory:

Voice of the lamb and dyed in his blood.

Last is Matthias
Red flow the banners ho!
Sing of the glory:

Twelve are the thrones in heaven.

(From *Children's Liturgies,* edited by Virginia Sloyan and Gabe Huck. The Liturgical Conference, 1970. Original source of the song "Red Flow the Banners Ho" unknown.)

E) **READING OF THE GOSPEL:** Luke 21:12-19

F) **HOMILY AND PRACTICAL ASPECTS:**
   The children should realize that saints are heroes, those who are great and admired by others. They are great because of their actions and lives. There are people in our lifetime whom we can imitate and admire because of their actions.

Some practical aspects for the week could be:

MONDAY — Go to the library and do some research on your patron saint.

TUESDAY — Try to list, with the help of your teacher, some heroes of our day.

WEDNESDAY — Make today a day of special prayer, asking God to make us faithful to his word like his saints were.

THURSDAY — Do not push anyone in line at the drinking fountain today.

FRIDAY — Ask your parents to let you celebrate the feasts of saints and heroes with a small party for the family.

G) **LITURGY OF THE EUCHARIST NOW TAKES PLACE:**

(All children dressed in costumes of saints are asked to come and stand around the altar.)

Prayer Over the Gifts

"Father, we present to you bread and wine. May you give us manna as we continue the work the saints have done before us in rebuilding your kingdom."

Prayer After Communion

"Father, we have received manna and are your children. May we go from this place to imitate your saints as they imitated your Son by revealing you to the world."

SUGGESTED SONGS FOR LITURGY FOR HALLOWEEN AND SAINTS' DAYS:

"Abraham, Martin, and John"

"Lonesome Valley"

"I Am the Resurrection"

"Let All the Earth"

"Into Your Hands"

"Day Is Done"

"Love Is Almost Worth the Dying"

"Born to Live and Die"

AFTER THE LITURGY

Banner — possible quotes:

1. The saints are the sinners who kept on trying.
2. Love is a season, may it last all your life.
3. The men who try to do something and fail are infinitely better than those who try to do nothing and succeed.

Application in School

The banner should be hung in its designated place, and the posters made and changed every day.

Biblical Readings

Some suggested readings for the week:

    MONDAY   — Romans 8:36

TUESDAY — Acts 9:16
WEDNESDAY — Luke 18:29
THURSDAY — Luke 9:24
FRIDAY — Luke 6:22

VARIATION

First Reading: Romans 8:34-39

NOTES:

_____
_____
_____
_____
_____
_____
_____
_____
_____
_____

A Liturgy for Pentecost

THEME

"Yahweh God fashioned man of dust from the soil. Then he breathed into his nostrils a breath of life, and thus man became a living being."

(Genesis 2:7)

ORDER OF CELEBRATION

A) Celebrant processes down the aisle and students sing "Blowing in the Wind."

B) **PENITENTIAL RITE:**

> That your Spirit will touch us today,
>> LORD HAVE MERCY

> That we may all be one,
>> CHRIST HAVE MERCY

> That your Spirit will put an end to war and hate,
>> LORD HAVE MERCY

C) **CELEBRANT READS AN APPROPRIATE PRAYER:**

> "Father, we thank you for the gift of your Spirit who stirs new life within us. May we always live a life filled with joy and love for our fellowman."

D) **FIRST READING:** Acts 2:1-4

E) **RESPONSORIAL:**

(A copy should be prepared for every student.)

WIND SONG

When the wind blows
The quiet things speak.
Some whisper, some clang,
Some creak.
Grasses swish.
Treetops sigh.
Flags slap
and snap at the sky.
Wires on poles
whistle and hum.
Garbage cans roll.
Windows drum.

When the wind goes —
suddenly
then,
the quiet things
are quiet again.

(Copyright © 1967 by Lilian Moore. From *I Feel the Same Way*. Used by permission of Atheneum Publishers.)

F) **GOSPEL READING:** John 15:20-27

G) **HOMILY AND PRACTICAL ASPECTS:**

"Spirit. Breath. Air. Wind. This liturgy is a celebration of a wondrous mingling of meanings. Spirit is not only like the air (invisible but necessary, sometimes awful in its power, often lovely in its gentleness) and breath (keeps us alive, gives us away, serves as a lifesaving technique), it is the air and the breath, the blowing and the breathing. Children should not have to unlearn a lot of confusing ideas about the Holy Spirit and the Trinity; rather they should, from their own limited experience, be able to see the way this teaching so naturally came about. We speak of the spirit of a team or a school, or the Spirit of Jesus, or of Jimmy or Sally. The way we know when some excitement, or some bad news is 'in the air'—like a storm—is the way we know how to speak of PENTECOST happenings."

(From *Children's Liturgies*, edited by Virginia Sloyan and Gabe Huck. The Liturgical Conference. "A Liturgy for Pentecost.")

The celebrant could make the children take deep breaths and hold them; make them blow, breathe quietly and pay attention to their breathing.

A balloon is passed down one row and the children are asked to put some of their spirit into the balloon. After the balloon is blown big enough, it is tied with a string that is long enough to tie to an object in the sanctuary.

After this a large disc, gaily decorated and containing candles (maybe red ones, one to represent each gift of the Holy Spirit), could be lit. A child from each class could do this. The children could sing again "Blowing in the Wind" or "The Spirit Is a-Movin'."

Some practical applications for the week could be:

MONDAY — During the day the students could make a small symbol of the Holy Spirit and wear it all week.

TUESDAY — Do library research on the gifts of the Holy Spirit and the Jesus Revolution. The teacher could read a story to the smaller grades.

WEDNESDAY — Pray in a special way that we may receive the Holy Spirit.

THURSDAY — Make a mobile with a symbol of the Holy Spirit to hang at home.

FRIDAY — Show a joyful spirit today by smiling even if you don't feel like it.

H) LITURGY OF THE EUCHARIST NOW TAKES PLACE:

Prayer Over the Gifts

"Father, we set before you bread and wine and a world which needs new life in you. Send your Spirit who helps us to say yes to your word."

Prayer After Communion

"Father, we have received your Son in Communion. Send your Spirit with the same touch that makes all things new."

SUGGESTED SONGS FOR LITURGY ON PENTECOST

"The Spirit Is a-Movin'"

"Speak to Me, Wind"

"Spirit of God" (From the album, *Joy Is Like the Rain.*)

"Blowing in the Wind"

"We Are One in the Spirit"

AFTER THE LITURGY

Banner — possible quotes:

1. Behold, I make all things new.
2. Breathe on me.
3. And the Spirit of the Lord filled him.

Application in School

The banner should be hung in its designated place, and the posters made and changed every day.

Biblical Readings

Some suggested readings for the week:

MONDAY — Genesis 2:7
TUESDAY — Acts 2:1-4
WEDNESDAY — John 15:20-27
THURSDAY — Hebrews 9:1-14
FRIDAY — 1 Timothy 4:1-16

NOTES:

A Liturgy on Witness

THEME

We all have to commit ourselves to spreading the "truth." The "truth" in school, on the playground, and at home. This was the job of the prophets in the Old Testament; but the job to witness goes on today. It is our job.

ORDER OF CELEBRATION

A) The celebrant processes down the aisle, while an appropriate song is sung.

B) **PENITENTIAL RITE:**

> For all the excuses we have used to keep from being witnesses of our faith,
>
> > LORD HAVE MERCY
>
> For our failure to extend you to others,
>
> > CHRIST HAVE MERCY
>
> For having spoken your message without love,
>
> > LORD HAVE MERCY

C) **AN APPROPRIATE PRAYER IS READ:**

> "Father, it is great to know all about you, but help us to show others your love."

D) **FIRST READING:**

A MAN AMONG MEN

Jesus himself, very different from the ascetic, John the Baptist, took part in banquets and let himself be abused as "a glutton and wine drinker" (Matthew 11:19).

He set a high value on marriage, reasserted its indissolubility, and was tenderly affectionate toward children.

He would not interfere in property matters, and proposed no new distribution of wealth.

He accepted the authority of the state and its right to levy taxes, and saw civic duties in a positive light.

Nor did Jesus want to cut his disciples off from the world. He did not want them, like the Essenes, to dissociate themselves from the people and found closed communities with a strict moral code.

He sent his disciples out into the world.

Peter, the brothers of the Lord, and the other apostles took their wives with them when they went to preach the gospel.

(Hans Kung, quoted in *Listen to Love*, by Louis Savary, S.J. Published by The Regina Press, Hicksville, N.Y. 11801. 1970.)

E) **GOSPEL READING:** John 1:1-8

F) **HOMILY AND PRACTICAL ASPECTS:**
In the liturgy of witness, we try to impress upon the children the fact that to be a Catholic Christian does not just mean going to church on Sunday; but religion must be important in all aspects of their lives— their friends, home and school, and, as they mature, it will hopefully be important in their political, social and economic lives.

Practical applications of the liturgy for the week could be:

MONDAY — Read the newspaper, find something good and cut it out, and bring it to school to share with other classmates.

TUESDAY — Read a story about Jesus and tell the story to your parents at home this evening.

WEDNESDAY — As a sign that you witness Jesus to other people, don't get into any fights today, at home or at school.

THURSDAY — Try to pay attention to the words that you say today when you pray.

FRIDAY — As true witnesses, make sure that you have done all the scripture readings for the week.

G) LITURGY OF THE EUCHARIST NOW TAKES PLACE:

Prayer Over the Gifts

"Father, accept this offering of ours, so that we may show our concern for you and others. We ask this through your Son, our Lord Jesus Christ. Amen."

Prayer After Communion

"Father, you have given us your Son. May we give ourselves to others."

SUGGESTED SONGS FOR LITURGY ON WITNESS

"Sing Out His Goodness"

"Turn Your Eyes"

"Amazing Grace"

"Witness Song"

"Joy, Joy, Joy"

"Halleluiah, Gonna' Sing All About It"

"Praise Him"

AFTER THE LITURGY

Banner — possible quotes:

1. There's work to be done before the kingdom can come.
2. You have the light, what are you doing with it?

Application in School

1. The banner should be hung in its designated place, and the posters made and changed every day.
2. The bulletin boards could be decorated with the good news clippings.

Biblical Readings

Some suggested readings for the week:

MONDAY — Matthew 3:16-17 and 1 John 5:6-10

TUESDAY — Acts 1:6-8 and Luke 6:13-15
WEDNESDAY — 1 Corinthians 1:27-31
THURSDAY — Luke 5:10-11 and 27-28
FRIDAY — Luke 18:22-30

VARIATIONS

First Reading: Isaiah 49:6

Gospel Reading: Matthew 5:14 or Mark 16:15

NOTES:

A Liturgy on Prejudice

THEME

Today we want to think about prejudice. Prejudice is hatred or unreasonable judgment made about someone or something, before all the facts are known. Perhaps we have been guilty of prejudice toward races, students and teachers. We want to help you overcome your prejudices.

ORDER OF CELEBRATION

A) The celebrant does not process up the main aisle; he begins immediately with the penitential rite.

B) **PENITENTIAL RITE:**

    For those sins which have harmed the dignity of others,

        LORD HAVE MERCY

    For participating in the social sins of our town that have kept minority groups in bondage and oppression,

        CHRIST HAVE MERCY

    For our indifference to others, especially students and teachers whom we don't know so well,

        LORD HAVE MERCY

C) **CELEBRANT READS AN APPROPRIATE PRAYER:**

"Father, why do people hate other people because of their skin, race or religion? In this celebration, help us to see that all the world needs to have is love."

D) **FIRST READING:**

(Guitars will play "Blowing in the Wind," and everyone will hum during the first reading.)

I HAVE A DREAM

I say to you today, my friends, that in spite of the difficulties and frustrations of the moment I still have a dream. It is a dream deeply rooted in the American dream.

I have a dream that one day this nation will rise up and live out the true meaning of its creed: "We hold these truths to be self-evident, that all men are created equal."

I have a dream that one day on the red hills of Georgia the sons of former slaves and sons of former slaveowners will be able to sit down together at the table of brotherhood.

I have a dream that one day every valley shall be exalted, every hill and mountain shall be made low, the rough places will be made plain, and the crooked places will be made straight, and glory of the Lord shall be revealed, and all shall see it together.

This is our hope. This is the faith with which I return to the South. With this faith we will be able to hew out of the mountain of despair a stone of hope. With this faith we will be able to transform the jangling discords of our nation into a beautiful symphony of brotherhood.

(Martin Luther King, Jr.)

E) **GOSPEL READING:** Matthew 7:1-5

F) **HOMILY AND PRACTICAL ASPECTS:**

Prejudice—"Nigger," "Spic," "Polack." The purpose of this liturgy is to instill into the child the fact that prejudice, bigotry and hatred do exist, and the only way to put an end to it is not by tolerating others, but by accepting them for what they are.

Some practical aspects of the liturgy could be:

MONDAY	— With the help of your teacher, look for some news account about prejudice.
TUESDAY	— Discuss this reading at home with your parents.

WEDNESDAY	— Try to be kind and friendly to the new people in school, both students and teachers.
THURSDAY	— Say something good about someone who annoys you.
FRIDAY	— Don't make fun of anyone today.

SUGGESTED SONGS FOR THE LITURGY ON PREJUDICE

"Blowing in the Wind"

"We Shall Overcome"

"It's a Long Road to Freedom"

"Battle Hymn of the Republic"

"Declaration of Independence" (Fifth Dimension)

"What Color Is God's Skin?"

AFTER THE LITURGY:

Banner — possible quotes:

1. Prejudice is the child of ignorance.
2. God is color-blind.

Application in School

The banner should be hung in its designated place, and the posters made and changed every day.

Biblical Readings

Some suggested readings for the week:

MONDAY	— 1 Timothy 5:21
TUESDAY	— Matthew 25:40
WEDNESDAY	— Matthew 7:1-5
THURSDAY	— Luke 6:22-24
FRIDAY	— 1 John 3:10-24

VARIATION

First Reading: John 3:10-18

NOTES:

A Liturgy on Peace

THEME

Today we want to think about peace. Peace is freedom from disagreement or quarrels. Peace is one of the effects of love. To have peace we need faith, good works and obedience to God. Sinners have no peace. For us the gospel message proclaims "the good tidings of peace."

ORDER OF CELEBRATION

A) The celebrant processes up the main aisle while students sing an entrance hymn.

B) **PENITENTIAL RITE:**

"If a bomb would drop tomorrow, it's because I hated my brother."

LORD HAVE MERCY

That peace begin in me,

CHRIST HAVE MERCY

That we will see peace in our day,

LORD HAVE MERCY

C) **CELEBRANT READS AN APPROPRIATE PRAYER:**

"Father, press us until we long for peace and until we are willing to pursue it."

D) **FIRST READING:** Ephesians 2:11-18

E) **GOSPEL READING:** John 14:27-31

F) **HOMILY AND PRACTICAL ASPECTS:**
We should try to help the students to realize that peace does not mean only an end to war, but the acceptance (love) of self and acceptance (love) of their brothers (fellow students)—no matter what are his beliefs, color, looks, mannerisms, ideas and ideals. In other words, acceptance and love of the other person. If you don't do it now, you're never going to. Or, will we continue to wallow in the mire of selfishness?

Some practical applications of the liturgy may be:

MONDAY — Wear your peace emblems this week.
TUESDAY — If someone tries to start an argument or a fight, don't take part.
WEDNESDAY — Let another member of the family look at his favorite television program.
THURSDAY — Say a special prayer today for peace.
FRIDAY — For the sake of peace, try to behave in class today.

G) **LITURGY OF THE EUCHARIST NOW TAKES PLACE:**

Offertory Procession:
Everyone processes to the altar to pick up a "peace symbol" and returns to his pew and pins it on.

Prayer Over the Gifts

"Father, accept this offering of the people dedicated to you and grant your Christian community 'peace.'"

Prayer After Communion

"Father, you are the author and lover of peace. Give us the peace of your Son so we may bring it to all men. We ask this through Christ our Lord. Amen."

SUGGESTED SONGS FOR LITURGY ON PEACE

"Gift of Peace"

"Peace I Leave With You"

"Shalom, O My Friends"

"Sing Praise to the Lord"
"Shout Out Your Joy"
"Great Mandala" (Peter, Paul and Mary)

AFTER THE LITURGY

Banner — possible quotes:

1. Be at peace, the Lord God is with you.
2. May the peace of Christ disturb you.
3. True peace is not merely the absence of tension, but it is the presence of justice and brotherhood.
4. The price of peace is love.
5. Spirit of peace, renew our world.

Application in School

The banner should be hung in its designated place, and the posters made and changed every day.

Biblical Readings

Some suggested readings for the week:

MONDAY — John 20:19-26 and 14:27
TUESDAY — Luke 23:36-43 and 3:48
WEDNESDAY — Mark 5:25-34
THURSDAY — Luke 19:38-40
FRIDAY — Romans 1:1-7 and Philippians 4:7-9

NOTES:

A Liturgy for Beginning School

THEME

Welcome to the new school year of (........). Welcome to all new students and teachers and priests in our school. Vacation is a time of rest, freedom from work and study. Today we wish to begin another year of awareness, understanding and growth. Together, let us celebrate this new school year.

ORDER OF CELEBRATION

A) The celebrant processes down the main aisle, while students sing an appropriate hymn.

B) **PENITENTIAL RITE:**

> For enjoying our summer vacation,
>> LORD HAVE MERCY
>
> For the time we spent reviewing what we learned last year,
>> CHRIST HAVE MERCY
>
> For the times we thanked you for our family and friends this summer,
>> LORD HAVE MERCY

C) **CELEBRANT READS AN APPROPRIATE PRAYER:**

> "Well, Father, summertime is over. It's time to get back to the books and our friends at school. May we learn to share and grow through

this coming year and enjoy experiences of life which will greatly change us. This we ask through Christ, our Lord. Amen."

D) **FIRST READING:**

People, like islands, need bridges—a way to cross over . . . speak . . . reach . . . see—over all that dead water. It is the only way, because people aren't people, not real people, without that bridge. The only action, the only real action, takes place on the bridge "between people." So, if I wait, you wait, everyone waits.

When I don't start, you don't start. Nobody arrives. No builders, no bridges. The meaning of the world doesn't change; it always stays the same, same hopes, same challenges, same tragedies, same fears and victories. What does change is my involvement with it, my awareness, my understanding, my growth. And growth is only the deepening of what passes between the world and me.

(Reprinted with permission from *Don't Just Stand There!* by Earnest Larsen, C.SS.R. © 1969 Liguorian Books, Liguori, Mo. 63057.)

E) **GOSPEL READING:** Matthew 7:7-11

F) **HOMILY AND PRACTICAL ASPECTS:**

Here we go again. School is a place for the student to learn how to get along with others, to work with others, to communicate with others, and all this is achieved through his studies.

Some practical applications of the liturgy may be:

MONDAY	— Get your name tag today during offertory procession and wear it all week.
TUESDAY	— Introduce yourself to new students and teachers. Share with your friends the good times you had this summer.
WEDNESDAY	— Write a letter to God thanking him for the wonderful summer you had and all the nice things you did.
THURSDAY	— Say some special prayers today in school, asking the Holy Spirit to help you with your schoolwork, to help you study, and to understand what you are doing.
FRIDAY	— Share with your mother and father all the things that you did in school this week.

G) **LITURGY OF THE EUCHARIST NOW TAKES PLACE:**
While an offertory hymn is being sung, the students are asked to come forward and get name tags. When they get back to school, they can mark their names on them and wear them. *(Celebrant may be seated until the procession is over.)*

Prayer Over the Gifts

"Father, accept our offering of bread and wine. With them, we offer you ourselves and all our work for the coming year. May they truly be signs of our community."

Prayer After Communion

"Father, may the meal we shared today bring us the greatest form of learning—love for others."

SUGGESTED SONGS FOR LITURGY ON BEGINNING SCHOOL

"The King of Glory"

"New Creation"

"God Made the World"

"Lord of the Dance"

"Love Is Almost Worth the Dying"

"Today"

"The Mass Is Ended"

"Take Our Bread"

"I Can See It"

"To Be Alive"

"Bridge Over Troubled Waters"

AFTER THE LITURGY

Banner — possible quotes:

1. When you're average, you're as close to the bottom as you are to the top.
2. Things go better with love.
3. Education is man's going forward from cocksure ignorance to thoughtful uncertainty.

Application in School

1. The banner should be hung in its designated place, and the posters made and changed every day.

2. The celebrant, at recess time on the first day, should go out on the school grounds and meet all the new students.

Biblical Readings

Some suggested readings:

MONDAY — John 5:19-30
TUESDAY — Romans 8:28-30
WEDNESDAY — Galatians 6:1-10
THURSDAY — Colossians 3:16-17
FRIDAY — 2 Corinthians 16-18

VARIATION

First Reading: Philippians 2:12-18

Name Tags—
Before Mass, the teachers prepare the name tags of the children. At the time designated by the celebrant, the teachers come up and get the name tags and give them to the children. The children pin them on. At Communion time the celebrant calls each child by name as he receives Communion.

NOTES:

A Liturgy for Teachers

THEME

Teachers are those dedicated people who help others to learn and understand their studies. The bible says that "those who instruct many in virtue will shine as bright stars for all eternity." Today we want to show our appreciation for our teachers by remembering them in a special way in our liturgical celebration.

ORDER OF CELEBRATION

A) The celebrant processes down the main aisle of the church while the students sing an appropriate hymn.

B) **PENITENTIAL RITE:**

    For not taking time to thank you for our teachers,

        LORD HAVE MERCY

    For not obeying our teachers,

        CHRIST HAVE MERCY

    For the love and concern our teachers show,

        LORD HAVE MERCY

C) **AN APPROPRIATE PRAYER IS READ:**

"Father, Jesus is often called Teacher. We pray for our teachers that they will not grow weary of questions or lose the joy of sharing knowledge with us."

D) **FIRST READING:**

WISDOM CAME TO ME

Wisdom is radiant and unfading, and she is easily discerned by those who love her, and is found by those who seek her. She hastens to make herself known to those who desire her.

He who rises early to seek her will have no difficulty, for he will find her sitting at his gates. To fix one's thought on her is perfect understanding, and he who is vigilant on her account will soon be free from care, because she goes about seeking those worthy of her, and she graciously appears to them in their paths, and meets them in every thought.

The beginning of wisdom is the most sincere desire for instruction, and concern for instruction is love of her, and love of her is the keeping of her laws, and giving heed to her laws is assurance of immortality, and immortality brings one near to God; so the desire for wisdom leads to a kingdom.

(Wisdom of Solomon 6:12-20, quoted in *Listen To Love* by Louis Savary, S.J. New York, Regina Press, 1971.)

E) **GOSPEL READING:** Luke 20:20-26

F) **HOMILY AND PRACTICAL ASPECTS:**

This liturgy is to help students understand the role of teachers in their lives. Teachers are not computers that we go to for all the answers; they are there to help students to grow intellectually, emotionally, physically, and spiritually. They are guides for students.

Some practical aspects for the week may be:

MONDAY	— Compose a poem for your teacher.
TUESDAY	— Try not to talk out of turn in class today.
WEDNESDAY	— The class should say a special prayer for teachers today.
THURSDAY	— Bring your teacher some flowers, or anything else that you want to create.
FRIDAY	— Thank the priests, for they are your teachers also.

G) **LITURGY OF THE EUCHARIST NOW TAKES PLACE:**

A child from every grade is asked to come forward to the microphone and present his teacher with a corsage.

The teachers are asked to remain standing in the middle aisle until all teachers have received their corsages. The teachers will then accompany the celebrant and stand around the altar for the liturgy of the Eucharist.

(On this day volunteers could assist by replacing the teachers if the principal does not care to have the student body remain alone in the pews.)

Prayer Over the Gifts

"Father, we receive so much from you and those who teach us. Accept this bread and wine as a sign of our thanks."

Prayer After Communion

"Father, may we receive the gifts of your Son and our teachers with diligence and joy, and share them with others."

SUGGESTED SONGS FOR LITURGY FOR TEACHERS

"Trust and Obey"

"Service"

"Tell the Wind"

"And I Will Follow"

"Day Is Done"

AFTER THE LITURGY

Banner — possible quotes:

1. Learning is an ornament in prosperity, a refuge in adversity and a provision in old age.
2. A little knowledge that acts is worth infinitely more than much knowledge that is idle.

Application in School

The banner should be hung in its designated place, and the posters changed every day.

Biblical Readings

Some suggested readings for the week:

MONDAY — Matthew 5:21-49
TUESDAY — Luke 4:42-44
WEDNESDAY — Matthew 11:25-30
THURSDAY — Luke 4:34-37
FRIDAY — Luke 9:57-62 and 14:25-33

NOTES:

_____
_____
_____
_____
_____
_____
_____
_____
_____
_____
_____

A Liturgy for Discovery

THEME

When we "discover" something it becomes real for us. The greatest reality in our life should be the love of God and our neighbor. If we have not done so before, let us today try to discover God in our neighbor.

ORDER OF CELEBRATION

A) The celebrant processes down the aisle of the church while the students sing an appropriate hymn.

B) **PENITENTIAL RITE:**

    For not realizing the gospel message sooner,

        LORD HAVE MERCY

    For not doing something about those poorer than we,

        CHRIST HAVE MERCY

    For not seeing the beauty of God,

        LORD HAVE MERCY

C) **AN APPROPRIATE PRAYER IS READ:**

    "Father, you know what we found out, that it was easy to hear your gospel but difficult to live it. May we do something about the people poorer than we—those not well educated, housed, heated, fed, cared for or loved."

D) **FIRST READING:**

IT'S FREE

It's free.

It is tuitionless and undiscriminatory.

It has sharp points and smooth corners.

It smells and feels and sounds and is.

It is all colors and everywhere.

It forces thinking by never explaining itself.

It is why every boy was born and what he was born for.

It is learning.

>When a light goes on in a human mind,
>
>who has flicked the switch?
>
>When that switch is on, what will keep it on?
>
>What happens then?
>
>Where will it lead?

Is it limitless? — this magical process

that is

Discovery

(As quoted in Shaping of a Self, Louis M. Savary,
Jane Carter and Charles Burke,
St. Mary's Press, Winona, Minnesota, 1970.)

E) **GOSPEL READING:** John 1:9-14

F) **HOMILY AND PRACTICAL ASPECTS:**

The purpose of this liturgy is not to emphasize land or space explorations, but to enable the child to discover the beauty of other people. Discovery is "beyond the surface." It is the realization that we have a potential to change the present situation in which we live and thus affect the world, to make it a better place for all men to live.

Some practical aspects for the week could be:

MONDAY	— At recess time, while playing, try to discover something good about a friend that you may have overlooked.
TUESDAY	— During art period this week, create a work that expresses your idea of "discovery."

WEDNESDAY — Pray and ask God today to help you understand the gospel messages that you read every day.

THURSDAY — With your teacher's help, see if it is possible to discover a gospel message in a song.

FRIDAY — Share your ideas of discovery with your parents tonight.

G) **LITURGY OF THE EUCHARIST NOW TAKES PLACE:**

Prayer Over the Gifts

"Father, accept these gifts and help us to live that *one* commandment to love with all our hearts, souls and strength."

Prayer After Communion

"Father, we have discovered your Son, ourselves and others in the breaking of the bread. May we take leave, and live your gospel."

SUGGESTED SONGS FOR LITURGY FOR DISCOVERY

"New Creation"

"Of My Hands"

"I Am the Resurrection"

"Yes, Lord"

"Pause a While"

"The Lord Is My True Shepherd"

"Glory to God on High"

AFTER THE LITURGY

Banner — possible quotes:

1. The wonder of God's love.
2. I have found a friend.
3. Love is discoveries without end.

Application in School

The banner should be hung in its designated place, and the posters changed every day.

Biblical Readings

Some suggested readings for the week:

MONDAY	— John 14:8-11
TUESDAY	— Matthew 24:26-36
WEDNESDAY	— Titus 2:11-14
THURSDAY	— Titus 3:4-7
FRIDAY	— John 3:2-8

VARIATIONS

First Reading:

The art of awareness is the art of learning how to awaken to the eternal miracle of life with its limitless possibilities.

It is searching for beauty everywhere, in a mountain, a machine, and a symphony.

It is developing a sense of oneness with all life.

It is being observant to all that goes on around you.

(Peterson, Wilfred. Quoted from *The Beauty of Easter*. Hallmark Cards, Inc. Kansas City, Missouri. 1968.)

(This poem could be read after the introduction of the liturgy.)

First Reading: Revelation 2:1-4

NOTES:

A Liturgy on Receiving-Accepting

THEME

Today we want to think about all the gifts we have received from God and from other people.

ORDER OF CELEBRATION

A) The celebrant processes down the main aisle of the church while the students sing an appropriate hymn.

B) **PENITENTIAL RITE:**

>   For receiving and not giving thanks,
>
>   > LORD HAVE MERCY
>
>   For receiving and not sharing,
>
>   > CHRIST HAVE MERCY
>
>   For accepting whatever comes our way,
>
>   > LORD HAVE MERCY

C) **CELEBRANT READS AN APPROPRIATE PRAYER:**

>   BEAUTY
>
>   The beauty in the world lies in its love. If there were no love there would be no beauty.
>   God is love, therefore the universe is beautiful.

Think of a clear crisp night after a sudden rainfall.
Feel the cool breeze on your warm cheeks.
Taste the freshness of the night in your lungs, and look with your eyes at the marvels above.
The sky so dark, the stars so bright, and the moon with its mystic radiance glows.
And think of the one who created all this.
How magnificent He must be, beyond our comprehension.

The waves roll and smash themselves into nothing as they crawl upon the beach.
Yet sea and sky seem to fuse into one at the farthest point; wherever that may be.
The bright sun reflecting across the glassy water, spitting the blue into two converging masses.
The loud but pleasing thunder as the waves collide among the smooth time-worn rocks.
The foam bubbling over like a giant sea monster emerging from beneath the surface and spreading out to swish between your toes.
And think of the one who created all this.
How magnificent He must be, beyond our comprehension. . . .

In the straw lay a babe, a weak and tender bundle of love—the creation must be beautiful; looking so simple yet so complete, so perfect.
And God chose to reveal Himself in the manger.
He came so humble, so common, so simple, yet he came to die that we might know true beauty.
And this beauty was His love for us, and think of the one who did this for us.
How magnificent He must be, beyond our comprehension, but our friend.

(From *Right On!* by Glen Bayley, *The Street People,* American Baptist Board of Education and Publication, Valley Forge, Pa. 1971. Used by permission.)

D) **FIRST READING:** Romans 11:33-36

E) **GOSPEL READING:** John 16:20-24

F) **HOMILY AND PRACTICAL ASPECTS:**

Receiving implies *thanks*. We hope to show students that thanks is a necessary response to receiving. Thanks must go beyond mere words.

Some practical aspects for the week could be:

MONDAY	—	Try to be especially thankful this week when people do things for you.
TUESDAY	—	Share something you have with someone else.
WEDNESDAY	—	Try not to complain about the unpleasant things you have to do today.
THURSDAY	—	Thank God today in prayer for all he has given you.
FRIDAY	—	Thank your parents for one thing they have given you this week.

G) **LITURGY OF THE EUCHARIST NOW TAKES PLACE:**

Prayer Over the Gifts

"Father, receive these gifts of ours. They are signs of your receiving us."

Prayer After Communion

"Father, we have received your Son and accepted one another in this breaking of the bread. May we always be thankful for these gifts."

SUGGESTED SONGS FOR LITURGY ON RECEIVING - ACCEPTING

"Today"

"Lord of the Dance"

"Day Is Done"

"Shalom"

"The Mass Is Ended"

"Scarborough Fair"

AFTER THE LITURGY

Banner — possible quote:

We must accept the things we cannot change.

Application in School

The banner should be hung in its designated place, and the posters changed every day.

Biblical Readings

Some suggested readings for the week:

MONDAY — Matthew 15:21-28
TUESDAY — Mark 10:46-52
WEDNESDAY — Luke 1:26-38
THURSDAY — John 9:6-39 or 9:35-39
FRIDAY — John 19:25-27

NOTES:

A Liturgy for the Closing of School

THEME

Today we wish to thank our priest and teachers for all the many kind things they did for us during this past school year, for the love we shared, for the trust we placed in one another, for our growth together.

We wish to remember all who will be leaving us at the end of this school year.

ORDER OF CELEBRATION

A) As the celebrant enters the church an appropriate hymn is sung.

B) **PENITENTIAL RITE:**

    For not giving ourselves completely to our schoolwork,

        LORD HAVE MERCY

    For all we learned and shared this year,

        CHRIST HAVE MERCY

    For all those we will never see again,

        LORD HAVE MERCY

C) **CELEBRANT READS AN APPROPRIATE PRAYER:**

    "Father, this school year we have shared life and lived life; together we have grown and loved. As we leave school today, may we bring these gifts to all we meet."

D) **FIRST READING:**

AWARE OF GOD'S GIFTS

Almighty God, Father of mercy, we thank you for all your goodness and loving kindness to us and to all mankind.
You create us, keep us and bless us in this life.
You showed your love for us, above all, by redeeming the world in Jesus Christ.
You bring us to life in your grace and fill us with the hope of glory.
Make us aware of all your gifts that we may truly appreciate them.
We want to praise you not only with our lips but in our lives, by serving you and by walking before you in kindness and justice each day of our lives, through Jesus Christ our Lord, to whom with you and the Holy Spirit, be all honor and glory, world without end. Amen."

(From *Listen to Love* by Louis M. Savary, S.J.
The Regina Press, Hicksville, N.Y. 11801. 1970.)

E) **GOSPEL READING:** Luke 1:68-75

F) **HOMILY AND PRACTICAL ASPECTS:**
Thoughts from the past year could be shared with the children. Perhaps now would be a good time to get a "feedback" on the liturgies that were used. Some practical aspects could be:

(1) Try to go personally to thank all the people who have helped you during this school year.
(2) Think of all the things that you learned this year and see if you have become a better person for it.
(3) Before you go to bed tonight, think of all the gifts God gave you this school year and thank him for them.
(4) Ask your teacher if she needs help putting things away for the summer.

G) **LITURGY OF THE EUCHARIST NOW TAKES PLACE:**

(If there is a graduating class, they are to come around the altar now.)

Prayer Over the Gifts

"Father, accept these gifts, the bread of our works, and the wine of our joy. We know that we are children of God loved by Jesus."

Prayer After Communion

"Father, we thank you for Jesus, ourselves and each other. May we continue to praise you throughout the summer."

SUGGESTED SONGS FOR LITURGY FOR THE CLOSING OF SCHOOL

"Day Is Done"

"Whatsoever You Do"

"And I Will Follow"

"Keep in Mind"

"Yes, Lord"

"Jesus Has Come"

"I Am the Resurrection"

"Peace, My Friends"

"Come, Let Us Go"

AFTER THE LITURGY

Banner — possible quotes:

1. To love someone is to invite him to grow.
2. See everything, overlook a great deal, improve a little.
3. Love is a season, may it last all your life.

Practical Application

MONDAY	— Clean all markings out of your textbooks.
TUESDAY	— Make a list of how you will review during the summer the subjects you learned during the school year.
WEDNESDAY	— Tell someone how great it has been to have known them during the year.
THURSDAY	— Thank your teacher for all the insights received during the year by giving her a gift or writing her a poem.
FRIDAY	— Write a letter to God, thanking him for making the school year a success.

Biblical Readings

MONDAY	— 2 Corinthians 13:11-13
TUESDAY	— Colossians 4:2-6
WEDNESDAY	— 2 Thessalonians 3:13-16
THURSDAY	— 2 Peter 3:17-18
FRIDAY	— Romans 16:25-27

VARIATION

First Reading: Philippians 1:1-11

NOTES:

IDEAS ANYBODY?

There are many more ways for children to experience God through the liturgy.

Listed on the following pages are some ideas you might like to develop — if "green is green"!

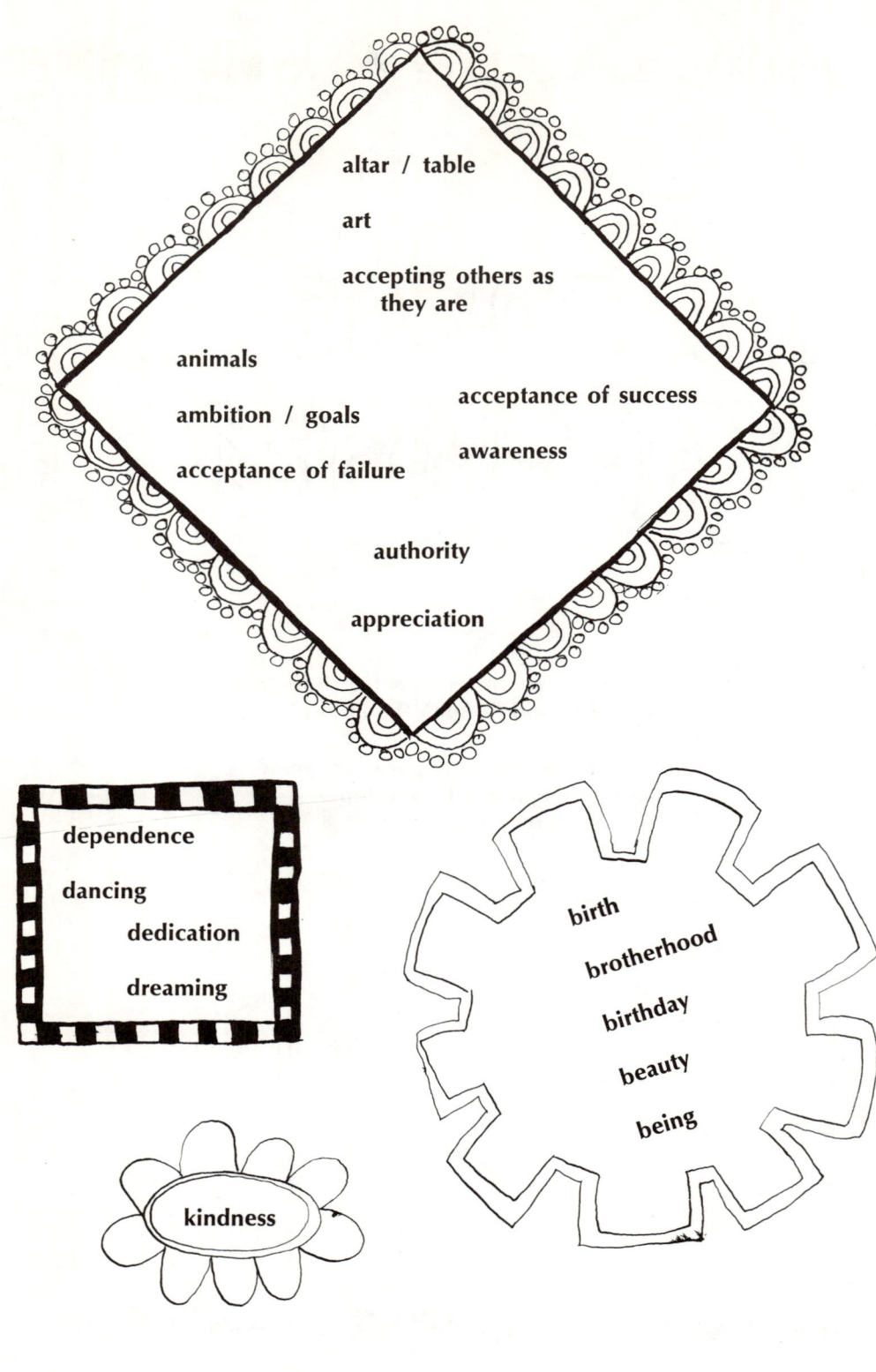

altar / table

art

accepting others as they are

animals

ambition / goals

acceptance of success

acceptance of failure

awareness

authority

appreciation

dependence

dancing

dedication

dreaming

birth

brotherhood

birthday

beauty

being

kindness

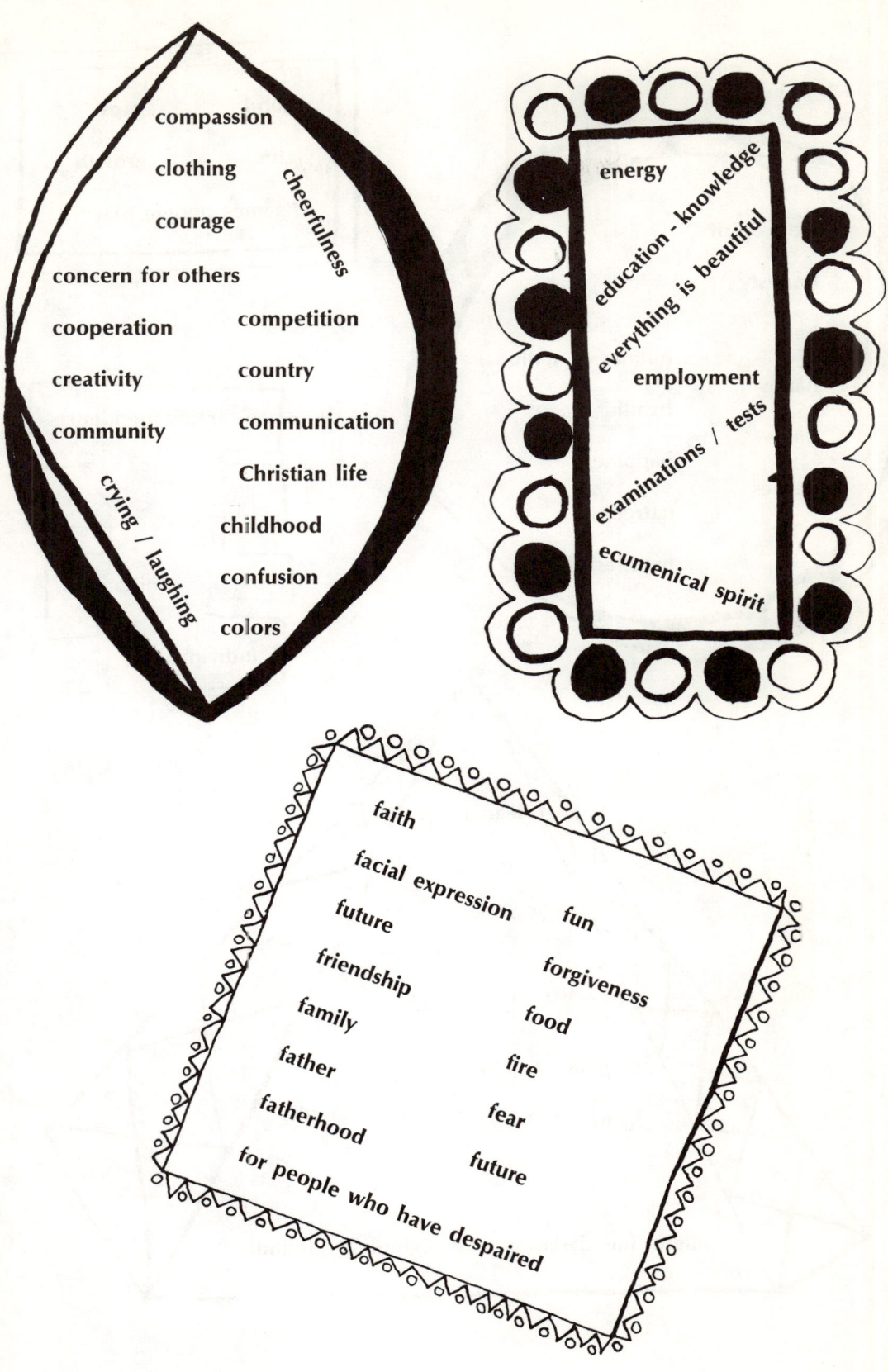

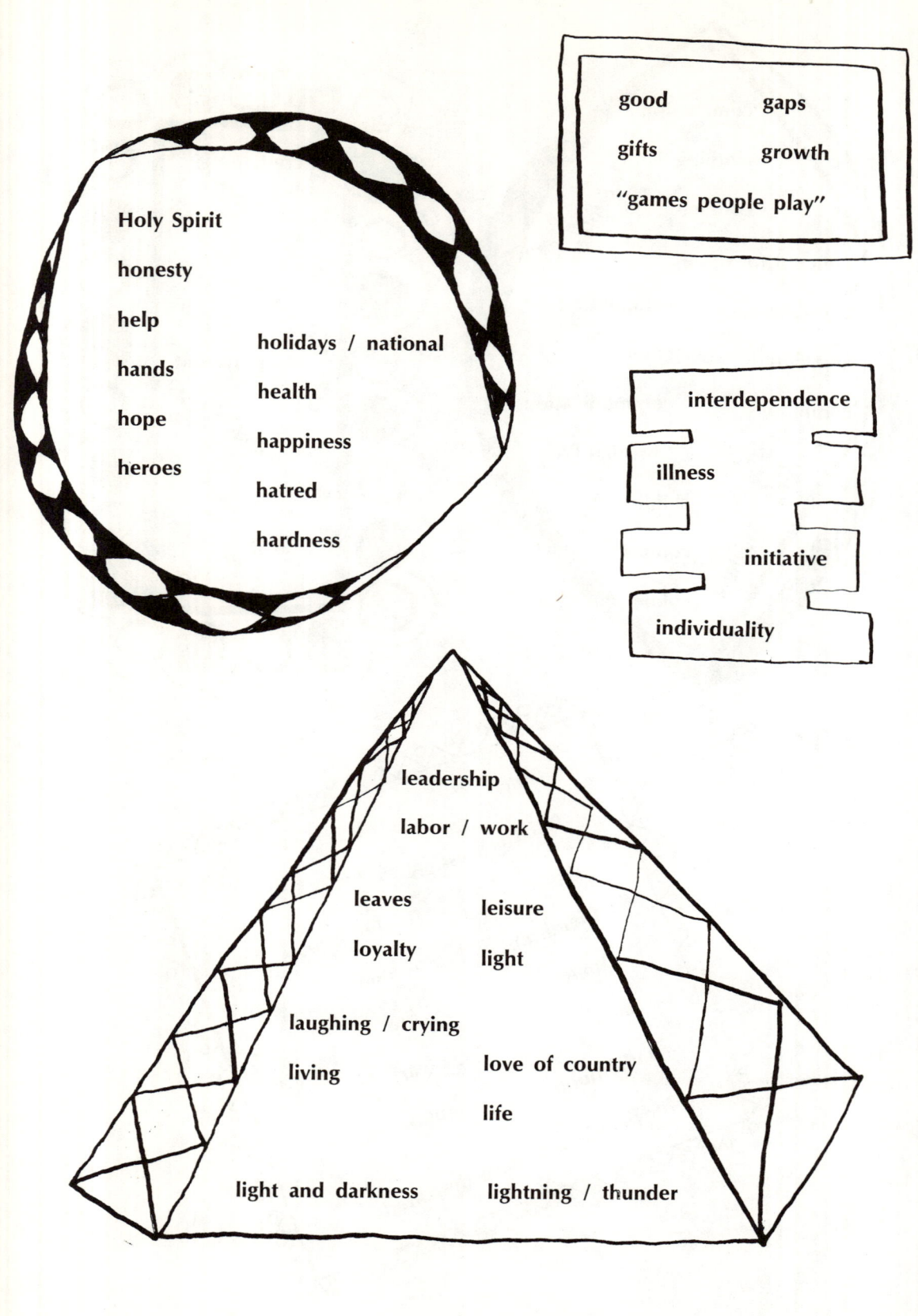

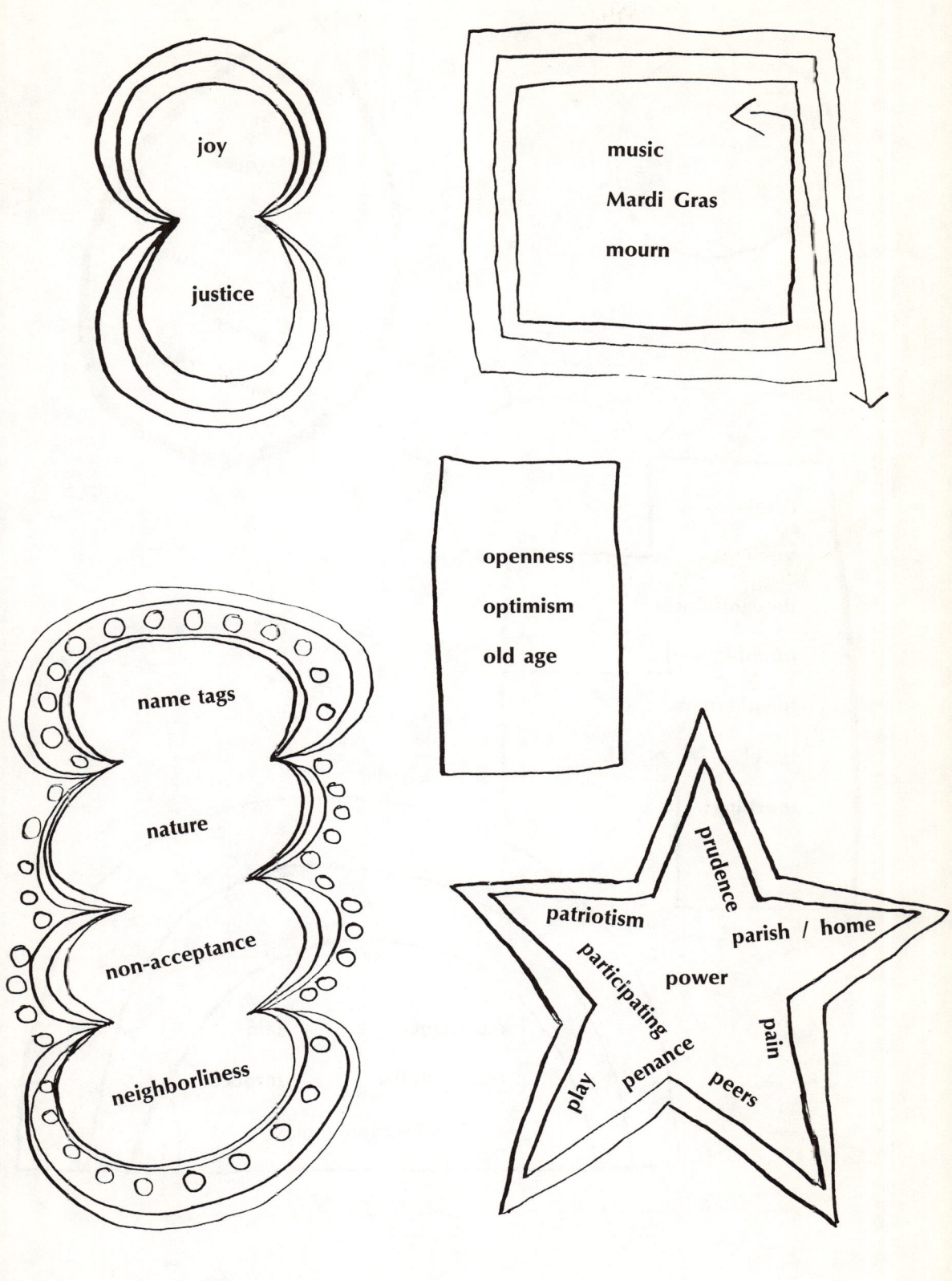

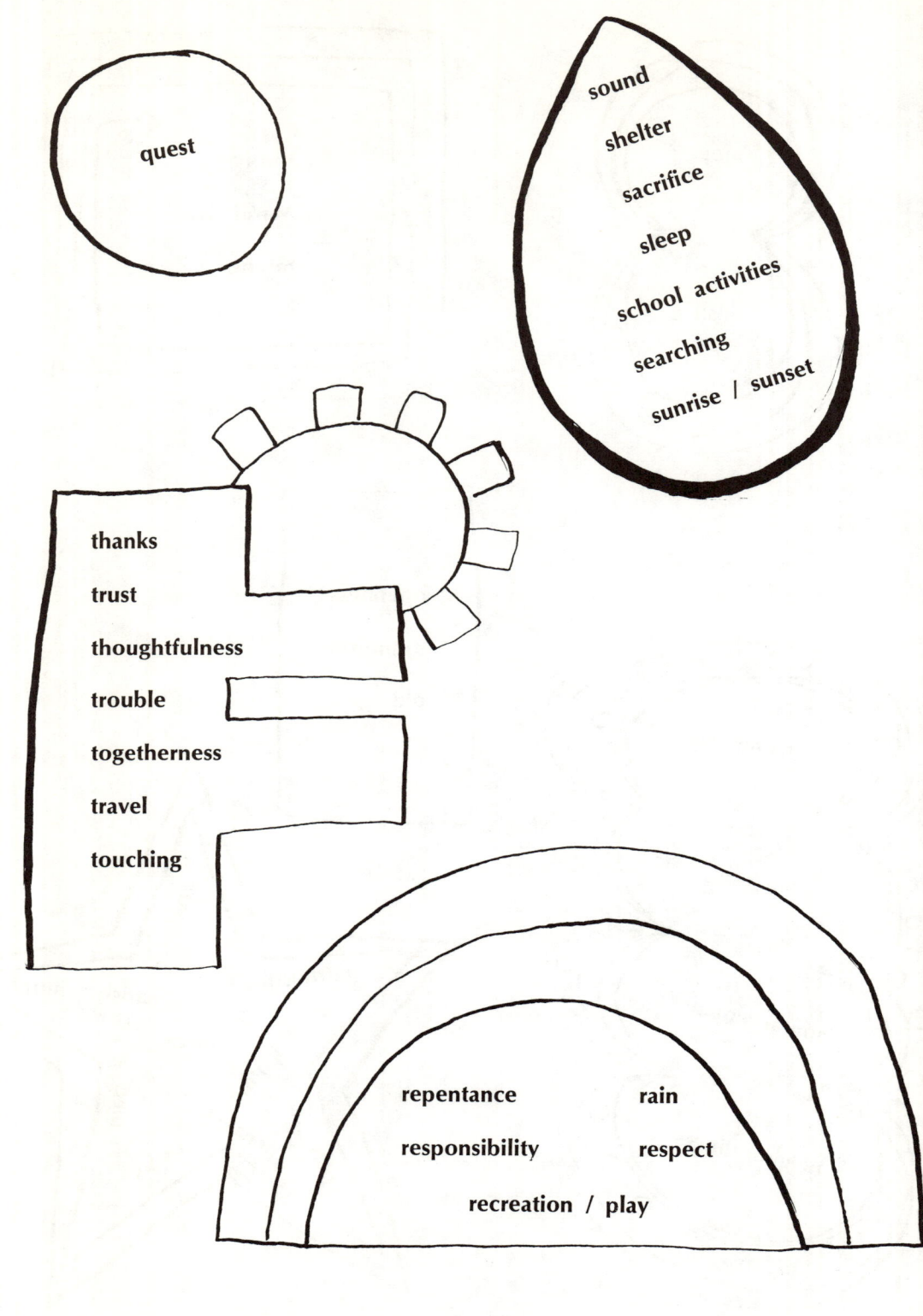

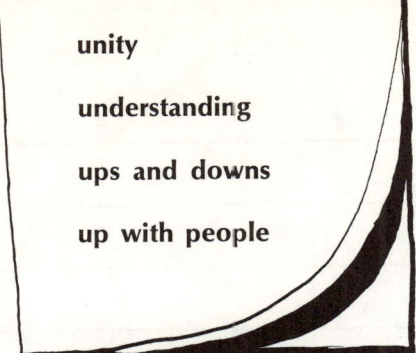

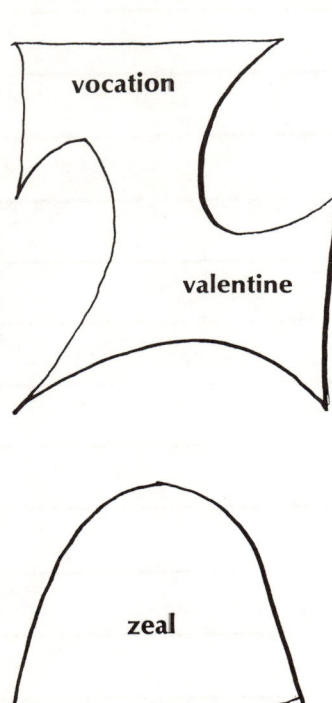
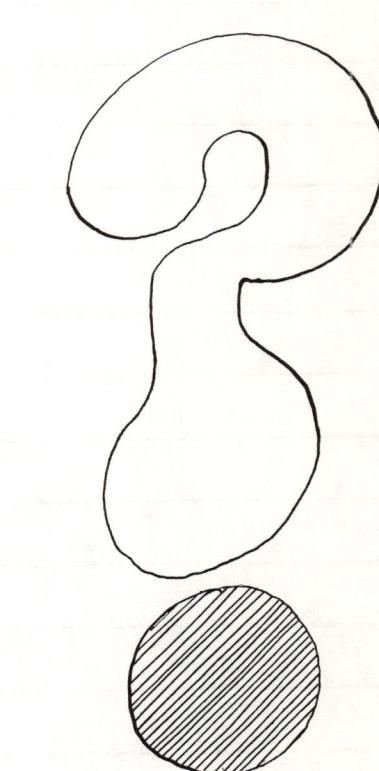
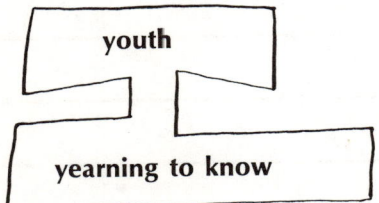

NOTES:

NOTES: